THROUGH A TEACHER'S EYES
THE MABEL LAWRENCE THOMAS STORY

FREDERICK D. JONES • SUE BOWRON

Frederick D. Jones • Sue Bowron

Praise for Mrs. Thomas from Former Students

I was in her first class at Franklin Parish Training School in 1963. She was very articulate and attractive. She was from south Louisiana and her diction and demeanor were fascinating to us as young boys. She was personable. In north Louisiana we were country, and she came with a southern diction and we enjoyed the change.

She was younger and very instrumental in shaping our thoughts and ideas about life and our future. She opened our eyes to science and biology. She had a unique ability to shed light on her subject matter.

We saw her as a person that we could not only talk to but also relate to as well. She had a love for kids. She enjoyed the craft of teaching but she was no nonsense.

A great educator! A great communicator! She valued people for who they were and not for the family they came from. She treated us all the same. She was not biased. Some teachers had built in biases but Mrs. Mabel L. Thomas had none. – **Van Hildren Brass, J.D., Pastor, Mount Zion Baptist Church, Rayville, Louisiana, Vice President of Louisiana Missionary Baptist Convention.**

She was loved by her students, coworkers, and administration. She was loved by everybody because she treated everybody the same. When students needed something, she would get it to them and not make an announcement to the world. – **Velma Neal Brown, MS +30, Assistant Principal, Winnsboro High School/Franklin Parish High School.**

Mrs. Thomas knew how to make every student feel that (s)he was her favorite! – ***Geneva*** **Jones Burrell, Executive Director, Destiny Now, Inc.**

I was in one of her very first biology classes. I remember thinking, 'This is a gorgeous lady.' After being her student for a while I realized that she was not only gorgeous outside but gorgeous inside. That made me want to be like her and to accomplish the things she had accomplished at a young age. I was impressed with her! At that time she was single and I felt if this attractive young woman could be this successful at an early age, I could do the same. – **Evelyn Cooper Carter, Employee Benefits Representative for General Motors Corporation, Retired.**

Mrs. Thomas is a lady, a dying breed. She is always impeccably dressed, with every hair in place. In the classroom, she was a calm and collected presence amid the undoubtedly stressful task of attempting to corral a rowdy crew of high school students. At the forefront of my memory is her soothing speaking voice. I loved to hear her talk. – **Tanya R. Cobb, BS, MS Nursing, Family Nurse Practitioner, Franklin Medical Center and Kevin W. Cobb, BS Finance, MBA, graduate of FBI Academy, Sheriff of Franklin Parish.**

Extraordinary teacher! I've learned a lot from her. She is like a second mother to me. I can go to her for advice. I just love her and to this day we still have a close bond. – **Shannon Credit, Custodian, Franklin Parish High School.**

My T-Mabel - She's the greatest! I admire her so much. She was the kind of teacher who would teach you if you wanted to learn. She was not the kind that would give you a grade because she admired you or if you were her friend. – Johnnie **Lamb, Machine Operator, Graphic Packaging.**

She's my favorite teacher! Mabel Thomas is a compassionate, caring, loving, sensitive, encouraging person. She has a very positive energy regarding education. She encouraged every student to reach for her or his potential and told them that they could be anything they wanted to be in life. She knew how to bring out the best in her students. – **Mary Simmons Locke, M.A., MBA, Department Chair of Computer Skills and Applications.**

She was a very caring, outstanding teacher that made you want to learn. She wrote on the blackboard and used the entire board! When I was Miss Franklin Parish Training School, we were poor and my mom was in Chicago. Mrs. Thomas gave me a gold suit. She dressed me up for Miss Franklin Parish Training School homecoming court. She wanted me to look good. – **Dorothy Parker-Swayzer, MS +30, Retired Teacher.**

Through a Teacher's Eyes

Mentor, friend, sister-in-law, encourager, intelligent, caring, responsible. She loves people. One of the best teachers I ever had. She was a driver! If you had it in you, she was going to get it out of you. She knew how to bring the best out of her students. – **Leola Allen Thomas, MS +30, Retired Teacher.**

Mabel Thomas is a pillar of our community and is the neighbor that everyone would love to have. She's always there when called upon, and she continues to be a guiding influence in the lives of our children, as well as a strong and active member of our community. We are truly blessed to have her among us. – **Lester Thomas, Jr., Chief of Police, Winnsboro, Louisiana.**

Very influential, very calm, very dignified person. One of the most friendly, loving, caring persons I've known. She made me feel that I was somebody. Louisiana was one of the last states to integrate and Franklin Parish was one of the last parishes to integrate. During this time Mrs. Thomas was a mediator, buffer, and a diplomat. She made everybody feel that education was the most important thing. – **Gene Thompson, Executive Director of Princess Theater, A Performing Arts Venue.**

As a teacher, she was very educated in the field of Biology. She assisted me financially. She's a friend, a confidant, a listener. When kids were in school and their parents could not financially help them, Mrs. Thomas would help. – **Jessie Marie Ignont White, Associate Degree in Nursing**

It was 1966 in Mabel Thomas' 10th grade biology class where I experienced a face to face encounter with a dead frog. I had no problem with the dead frog until my teacher told me I would have to dissect it. YUCK! She coached me and the rest of the class through it with educational excellence, beauty, and grace. Her consistency and dedication to teaching is an inspiration to us all. – **Marie Jones Williams, Underwriter for State Farm Insurance.**

One of my best teachers . . . very knowledgeable, intelligent, a no-nonsense teacher. She could convey. She knew how to get her message across. She made sure we did what we needed to do to succeed in life. She made sure we would reach our potential. – **Janice Harrington Winder, Ph.D., Vice Chancellor of Student Affairs, Southern University New Orleans, Retired.**

Through a Teacher's Eyes

Dedication

This book is dedicated to ALL the teachers from Fort Necessity School, Franklin Parish Training School, Winnsboro High School, and Franklin Parish High School. Finally, this book is dedicated to:

Beatrice Winters Jones
My Mother
June 9, 1919 – October 15, 2010
and
Mose Jones
My Father
October 12, 1920 - November 23, 2007
MY FIRST TEACHERS.

Frederick D. Jones

To Britton – Dreams really do come true.

Sue Bowron

Proceeds from this book will be donated to the Advocates of Christ Teen Law Awareness Programs.

Frederick D. Jones • Sue Bowron

Forward

As I entered high school in 1976, a shy and timid freshman, I met Mrs. Mabel Thomas who would impact my life in no small measure. More than a teacher, she soon became my mentor, role model, inspirer of dreams – my friend. To her, I became "Miss T" and to me, she became "Mrs. T." Her classroom was more than a classroom; it was a laboratory of sorts where Mrs. T worked her magic, molding futures, impacting lives – mine included.

If I were to focus on the one unique quality Mrs. T possessed, it would be her unique way of raising the average in the lives of her students. This was especially true in my own experience. She not only believed in me, but also empowered me to believe in myself. More than a teacher, she was an investor in the lives of her students.

In 1978, Mrs. T wrote in my yearbook that I was a "chubby, blue-eyed blond with a pretty smile" and dared to call me an "ideal student." I believe it was more her faith in what I could be than the fact that I was an ideal student at the time. She was generous with praise and had a way of reinforcing a positive self image. Soon, my shyness and timidity were displaced by a passion to achieve my potential and a confidence that I could do anything I dared to dream. Mrs. T was working her magic!

Through a Teacher's Eyes

In my sophomore year, Mrs. T had already decided that I was to be her successor. In my yearbook, she penned, "Let's not forget our plans," meaning I would replace her upon her retirement. She retired in 1992 and guess who should occupy Room 303 at Winnsboro High School the next school year? That's right, the "chubby, blue-eyed blond with a pretty smile."

In 1992, at a retirement tea in honor of Mrs. T, I read the following lines written by Perry Tanksley, which aptly capture the essence of this wonderful lady's influence on me:

> *Your faith was great*
> *Inspiring me to be*
> *Much more than I had planned . . .*
> *Your faith in me*
> *That in life could win*
> *Sure pulled the average up*
> *From what I might have been.*

Call it a gift or whatever, but Mrs. T, like a master potter, possessed the unique ability to mold her students into vessels of extraordinary utility. Somehow, she raised our level of desire. She has a gift for bringing out the best in people and helping them overcome their inhibitions and self-imposed limitations. She made you believe that the world is a stage designed just for you and her classroom was your dressing room – the place where you prepared yourself to take the world by storm. She looked for opportunities to improve her students and never failed to seize the chance to reinforce our self-confidence. I will always cherish her for that.

Mrs. T wrote me once saying, "I hope in some way that I have provided the proper encouragement and given you the best advice to help your years at Winnsboro High School, from start to finish, to be the most rewarding." She then quoted Henry Ford who said, "He is your friend who brings out of you the best that is in you." Many people talk about such friendship; Mrs. T defines it.

Also at her retirement tea, printed on a brochure were the words from a prayer written by Richard Cardinal Cushing of Boston, which ended with these words:

Dear God,
Help me to be a good sport in this game of life . . .
Help me study the Book, so I'll know the rules . . .
And when I finish the final inning,
I ask no laurels.
All I want is to believe in my heart
That I played as well as I could.

Mrs. T. has played well in this game of life. Many thanks go to my dear friend for her investment in my life and for caring enough to make a difference. She, indeed, pulled my average up from what I might have been.

Through a Teacher's Eyes

It is my distinct honor to contribute these words to this volume; though be assured, the half has not been told!

Theresa Heath Whistine
Former Winnsboro High School Teacher
Administrator for the Purpose Institute

Frederick D. Jones • Sue Bowron

Introduction

The whole world opened to me when I learned to read.
Mary McLeod Bethune

This is a story of a teacher whose classroom was more than a classroom; it was a place where lives were transformed and students who had never dreamed before were able to visualize and ultimately obtain a measure of success. The objective is to provide encouragement, inspiration, and hope to all parents and teachers to see beyond juvenile misconduct and to know that ONE word, ONE statement could cause the light to come on in a student's eyes.

As one of Mrs. Thomas' many pupils, I wanted to express my gratitude for her insight along my youthful mischievous path. As a student, I was envious of my friends who were getting higher marks. They were known as the "A" group and the "B" group. Even though I may have coolly mocked them, I secretly wanted to be in that group. I wanted to be out of the "C" group and moving into where I thought I belonged and needed to be. In this book I share insights and comments made by my teacher that were earth shaking and caused me to pause, regroup, and refocus my life.

One of the most difficult tasks in life is getting people to see themselves as God sees them. This difficulty is compounded when one is teaching teenagers who don't want to see their potential. This problem is as ancient as man.

When God led the Israelites into the Promised Land, Moses sent scouts ahead to see what the new land was like. The Bible tells us that some of the scouts were intimidated by what they saw reporting that there were giants living there. They said, *We seemed like grasshoppers in our own eyes, and we looked the same to them (*Numbers 13:33). They interpreted their own capabilities, not by what they were in God's eyes, but how they thought others saw them. They limited their own possibilities by not believing in their own God-given potential.

In *Through a Teachers Eyes* we will learn the principles of respect, determination, commitment, love, faith, and vision that Mabel Lawrence Thomas observed and taught, in turn giving insight, vision and hope to all of her students. What was it that Mrs. Thomas saw in her students that some others did not see that caused her to be known as "a great motivator," "the best teacher I ever had," and simply, "the greatest?"

Frederick D. Jones • Sue Bowron

Through a Teacher's Eyes is a tribute to a visionary teacher who touched my life and caused light to shine upon my pathway giving me the inspiration to reach beyond the "C" group into my life destiny.

Frederick D. Jones, J.D.
Director of Academic Success
Louisiana College Judge Paul Pressler School of Law

Through a Teacher's Eyes
The Mabel Lawrence Thomas Story

By

Frederick D. Jones

And

Sue Bowron

Cover design by Carole Magué-Lewis

Frederick D. Jones • Sue Bowron

1 – Transition

Pulling two more books off the bookshelf and stuffing them into a box, I was frustrated with the tedium of packing. I knew I was making a mess of things, just stuffing things into boxes as they came to me but I just wanted the job over with. Reaching for the packing tape, I folded the lids of the box down carefully and taped it up. I scrawled the unambiguous word *BOOKS* on the top, which only described their generic shapes, nothing about their uniqueness and purpose. I knew I would resent it later on when I had to find something in a hurry.

It was quiet all around me in the late afternoon as I sat down to sort through some papers on my desk. The semester was over and the students had left for the summer. A stack of cards from my farewell party lay in a heap and I picked them up and stuffed them unceremoniously into an empty box. The memory of the party played back in my mind with catered sandwiches and a large sheet cake with "Congratulations, Fred" in gold and black frosting in honor of the university's colors. I had been touched by the number of colleagues and friends who had squeezed into the small conference room and hallway to wish me well. I was surprised that some had come from so far away and by the affection expressed by some of my closest colleagues. My ten years teaching Business Law and Ethics in the School of Accountancy at Kennesaw State University had been the most satisfying time of my career.

Now I was packing up to take a job in Shreveport, Louisiana near my hometown of Winnsboro. The decision to make the change was filled with possibility and excitement but the actual leaving was a bit heart rending. Not only was I saying good-bye to my friends and colleagues, but I was also leaving a church and ministry I dearly loved. My oldest son lived in the Atlanta area and was struggling on and off with school, jobs, girls, and trying to find his footing as a young adult. We had been through some tough times together and I felt it was time to let this beautiful child stand on his own feet. I had provided a soft place to land for far too long. While I knew there was no statute of limitations on being Dad, I felt he had the inner strength to make it on his own if the safety net wasn't quite so close. I said a silent prayer, one that God had heard far too often, and sent my blessing through the air to my son.

Opening a desk drawer, I pulled out a fistful of papers and threw them into the box. A photograph fluttered onto the floor. I bent over to pick it up and my stomach was another reminder of indulging in a second piece of good-bye cake. I grunted the old man's sound as I picked up the photo and turned it over in my hands. It was a photo of me and my high school teacher. She was a short woman but she had me by the proverbial ear for as long as I can remember. I heard her voice in my mind, "Fred Jones, you're an embarrassment to the Jones family name!" I flinched just a bit as if I were still in her presence twenty years ago and then laughed. Even though I was more than a foot taller than she and was now an attorney with a Juris Doctor degree, a member of the Louisiana Bar and the United States Supreme Court Bar, a college instructor, an ordained minister, and a father of two grown sons, this little woman had the power to still make me sit up straight and listen.

Reaching over to take my degrees off the wall, I brushed the dust off the frames with my hand. A Bachelor of Arts in Pre-Law from University of Louisiana Monroe and my law degree from Southern University Law Center in Baton Rouge and now, I'm going to be a charter faculty member at the new Judge Paul Pressler School of Law in Shreveport. The thrill of the future shot through me. "How did this happen?" I wondered. For sure, they were achievements that went beyond my own talents and abilities. Others had a hand – my parents, my pastor, my siblings, but a lot of the shaping of expectations came from this little woman, this little teacher from Franklin Parish High School in Winnsboro, Louisiana who ruled with an iron fist. She never backed down, she never accepted excuses, she always expected the best, and she made me feel like I was her only student. Disappointing her was not an option, not one that I ever wanted to live through anyway. I realized, not for the first time, that I owed her more than my education. I owed a great quantity of my life to her because she taught more than biology. She taught me how to live beyond limitations. She made the impossible possible and it all began by putting one foot in front of the other.

Through a Teacher's Eyes

Mabel Lawrence Thomas - Biology and Science Teacher

I stared out the glass window that looked down on the atrium of the Coles School of Business and its contemporary beauty felt almost foreign in comparison to her bare functional classroom in Winnsboro. Here, I am the teacher with others beckoning for my expertise but there and then, I was a scrawny kid with a chip on my shoulder trying to be the tough guy. She introduced herself to the class and I watched her from the back of the classroom a lifetime ago through narrowed eyes. Standing erect, she looked like a fifth grader in a woman's dress. "I'm Mrs. Thomas," she said looking the students squarely in the eyes, "Mrs. Mabel Thomas and I'm your teacher." I didn't know then that she would change my life.

2 – Moving

Crossing the state line from Mississippi into Louisiana I slowed down a notch to keep within the speed limit. With every mile I had driven from Atlanta there was a change in feeling. As I hugged my son good-bye, there was regret in leaving him behind. As I passed the Church of the Apostles on Interstate 75, I already missed my friends that I worshipped with every week. Through the men's fraternity, Living Waters, I had met people from a wide diversity of circumstances. I quickly learned that misfortune and pain affected everyone and as I counseled with these men, I grew to accept and appreciate our differences. My own faith had grown considerably over the past five years under the ministry of our pastor, Dr. Michael Youssef. During this time I had confronted a lot of my own mistakes and felt that God had not only forgiven me, but also provided me with opportunities to help others.

Driving into the countryside west of Atlanta, my shoulders began to relax and my fingers tapped the steering wheel in anticipation. My old Toyota Avalon cruised through Alabama before I stopped for lunch. That car had over 350,000 miles on it, racked up during countless trips from Winnsboro to Atlanta. My mother had been ill for months and I wanted to be by her side as much as possible during her last days. This time together was a gift for both of us. I picked up speed for the afternoon drive into Mississippi. Rolling down the window, I got a blast of hot air rushing over my face and I leaned my elbow out the window slouching down in the seat with the highway stretching out in front of me.

Louisiana is home like in your bones home. You have to love it for what it is. It's a place of deep roots and long memories. Crossing the state line invoked images of my brothers and sisters. No longer little Frederick, I always felt like I had to take my place in line when I returned home. My family had lived in Franklin Parish for generations and it was little changed since my childhood. That's what made it so rich for me. The landscape was always the same. Flat stretches of scrubby grass fighting for a chance to grow in the dusty soil. Live oak trees clustering on the edges of plowed fields stubbornly refused to be tamed by local farmers. Houses with acre-sized yards lined up along the highway. Company parked in the front yard, never on the road. People dropped by and were always welcome. This was the land of sweet potatoes, collard greens, fried chicken, and warm embraces.

The tired grocery store with the cracked asphalt parking lot still kept watch by the highway coming into town. The Western Auto remained but the ice cream place was closed. It used to have one window for black customers and another one for white. It occurred to me that the ice cream must have melted while they tried to sort that issue out.

As I pulled into my family's homestead where I grew up, memories flooded over me. My sister, Emma Blackshire, had taken over my parents' home after they passed and she kept the place alive for the rest of us. The familiarity of the place hung on me like a loose suit. I had always loved coming home because here I was known for myself, not for my accomplishments or titles, but for my own being. If I had a sense of pride, I had nine sisters who would peel it off of me in a moment. The women in my family were like iced tea, sweet and strong, and they ruled over and cared for us all. We were fed, washed, rocked, scolded, and loved every day of our lives by a unified maternal force. I had accepted long ago that I would never be a big shot at home and it was a mistake to even try. It was a lesson in humility that chafed me in my earlier days but now one that I accepted gladly. My time in Atlanta had allowed me to establish my professional identity and now no matter how much ribbing my family gave me, I could accept it good-naturedly.

That evening I stretched out on the couch while Emma finished preparing dinner. I reached over into her bookcase and pulled out her high school yearbook. The picture of Franklin Parish High School looked like it could have been taken yesterday. It always surprised me how little things changed in Winnsboro while Atlanta experienced constant and sometimes frustrating growth. Landmarks were ever changing in Atlanta and the curving name-changing streets didn't help especially with the seemingly omnipresent name of Peachtree on every other building and street. The contrast between the two places played tricks on my mind. Winnsboro was comforting; Atlanta was challenging.

Turning the page I saw a picture of Emma with her cheerleading squad and their sponsor, Mrs. Thomas. She was shorter than most of the students but her face shone with pride as she stood among them. Emma was speaking to me and I realized she was standing over my shoulder looking at the yearbook. "I saw Mrs. Thomas just the other day at the grocery store," she was saying.

"Yes, yes," I responded pulling myself back to the present, "How was she?"

"Always the same," she said going back into the kitchen, "That woman never changes."

No, she doesn't, I realized and then I promised myself she would be among the first I would visit before starting my new position at Louisiana College. Dinner was ready and I was ready for it. I looked across the table at my sister and realized that she had Mrs. Thomas as a teacher as did seven of my other siblings. What an influence, I thought, and not just on me.

3 – Learning

Mrs. Thomas agreed to meet me the next week and I found myself choosing a newer shirt and giving my shoes a quick buffing before starting over to her house. I was excited and slightly nervous about seeing her. We had kept in touch over the years and I often visited her when I came home but I never lost the feeling of wanting to be at my best when I saw her. I chided myself, Fred Jones, you're a grown man. And then laughed and gave it up. It was what it was.

She met me at the door all graciousness and smiles. She had aged some but she hadn't lost her vibrancy and her quick mind. Her eyes were alive with inquisitiveness. She leaned forward and asked, "So tell me all about it." And I did. I told her how I had met the people who were starting the new law school through a friend and the plans for the new Shreveport campus. I explained the intricacies of obtaining the former Waggonner Building, a former federal courthouse complete with courtrooms, and how many students we expected. I told her about my role as the Director of Academic Success in the new school and my excitement on getting in on the ground floor of such a substantial endeavor.

I stopped for a breath and realized I had been talking non-stop but her face was still intent on mine, absorbing every word. "How did you know it was the right thing to do?" she asked. I leaned back and opened up my heart. I told her how I hadn't sought any of it but it just slowly unfolded to me. I had been happy as a lecturer of business law and ethics at Kennesaw State University but this new position had an allure. It wasn't that it was new even though that was intriguing in itself. It was the Christian emphasis that really captivated me. As a unit of Louisiana College, the law school would carry on its tradition to teach with a Christian perspective. I had felt for a long time that the law should not be used in an adversarial sense but undergirded with integrity. It should be used for justice, not for advantage. I told her I might be a bit naïve but that the law should bring out the best in society, not "the end justifies the means" approach that was so prevalent.

Her Mona Lisa smile made me wonder what she was thinking. I showed her my new jacket that the school had just given me with the law school crest. Its motto was in Latin, *Deus, Veritas, and Patriae.* She ran her fingers over the crest, "God, Truth, and Country," she said. "Yes," I responded and the words seemed hallowed between us.

"I feel like I belong there," I continued, "I feel like God wants me there. It really is a dream opportunity for me. I've always believed that the law and the ministry are one in the same. When I went to law school, I wanted to use my degree as a ministry tool. While I was at Southern, a few other law students and I started a group called The Advocates of Christ. I still lead it today. " She nodded in response but remained pensive.

I went on bursting with enthusiasm, "You know, the three original legal professions were medicine, ministry, and the law. Medicine heals the body. Ministry heals the soul, and law heals the community. I'm a community healer!"

Her smile broadened and she acknowledged, "Now, you're the teacher. I've learned something today."

I looked down at my feet, realizing I had been talking for far too long. "Why did you become a teacher?" I blurted out breaking the silence between us.

"Why . . . ," she paused and shrugged as if the answer were obvious, "Because I never wanted to do anything else. I always wanted to be a teacher – really, all of my life, ever since I can remember, probably since I was three years old."

"But, how did you know?" I pressed.

"I don't know how I knew," she said, "I just knew and I never doubted it. I didn't have to think it over. It was part of me ever since I was a little girl. I was the one who told my parents what I was going to do long before I was old enough to make any decisions about my future."

I looked into her face and began to realize that I was in the presence of a person who came into the world nearly completely made. My journey was a long process of self-discovery and self-mastery. I had always been interested in the law and in the ministry but thought they were two exclusive professions. It was only after I started my pre-law education that I could see that they could be blended. But sitting in front of me was a person who knew from the very early beginnings of her life what she wanted to do.

She could see my mind working and she smiled that Mona Lisa smile leaning back into her chair. Her manicured fingers rested on the arms and she closed her eyes briefly.

"It all started with my mother," she said.

"She called me Mabel because I was able. It was like a song when she stroked my hair and she told me so often that I was Mabel because I was able that it became part of me. It never occurred to me that I couldn't do anything or that I would fail at anything. I was able – what else would a Mabel be?" she smiled.

"I was born on a Friday morning on March 29 in 1940 in Charity Hospital on Tulane Avenue in New Orleans. I don't think Charity Hospital exists anymore. I was my parents' fourth child. It's funny but I was kind of a big baby. I weighed nine pounds and I think I was 14 inches long. I guess I wanted to get a good head start because I didn't finish up all that big!" she laughed at her own joke.

"My older brother was named Noles Lawrence, Jr. after my father and Julia was my oldest sister and my next oldest sister was called Lillie Rose, kind of after my mother who was Lillie Harriet. My parents got married in 1932 on November 12th. Remember, I always keep a list of family birthdays and anniversaries," she waved her hand dismissively.

"And they moved into a shotgun house in Oakville just outside of New Orleans. Nearly everybody lived in a shotgun house at that time. The first room was the living room, the second room was Mother and Father's room, the third room was for the girls and the fourth for the boys. The kitchen and dining room were at the end of the house. The outhouse was out back and we had a tin tub for baths. The boys would have to carry in water for baths. They hated it because they had to carry the water in and dump it out after but what could they do? It was their job. We had our jobs and they had theirs.

"We lived next door to a grocery store that was run by some white people and on the other side, our neighbors were Italian. Mrs. Salamoni would come over to sit and talk with my mother. She would talk to us like we were her own children. We called her our white grandmother. If we didn't listen to her, she would tell Mommy and then we would all be in trouble.

"Our home was the place for family gatherings. Everybody would bring something and we would have a feast. My mother always fed people, too. It seemed like every Sunday after church someone would show up at the house to eat. My brother James is two years younger than I am and he would always fuss and complain, 'I don't know why all those people come and eat up all the food. We're not going to have any food left and Mama isn't going to let us eat until they finish eating.' You see, Mama would serve company first and after they would leave, we would eat. James would be the first one to run into the kitchen and look in the pot to see if there was enough to eat and there always was."

Laying my head back on the back of the sofa, I settled in for a good story. I could practically smell the collard greens and cornbread.

"My father was a big tall man over six feet tall. His family was Mandingo from West Africa and he had coffee bean brown skin with a reddish color in his skin tone. He was Creole though, because somebody somewhere was French a long time ago. He looked different than other people but he was Daddy to us. He worked all the time. His birthday was on Christmas Day and he was born in 1913. His mother tried to call him "Noel" for Christmas but it was put down wrong on the birth certificate and so he became Noles."

"What about your mother?" I asked.

"She was beautiful," Mrs. Thomas lowered her eyes remembering. "Her father was Indian and I inherited a reddish color to my skin, maybe from my father or maybe from my grandfather. When I was little, my nickname was Red.

"My mother was always at home taking care of us. She was a great cook and she talked to us all the time. Whenever we came in, we had to give her a hug and a kiss and every night she kissed each one of us calling us by name. To this day, with my entire family, we hug and kiss everybody before we leave or go to bed. Some of the in-laws have a problem with it!" she laughed.

"My parents were very loving people," she continued and then almost in a whisper she said, "I miss them."

Mrs. Thomas cleared her throat, "You know, I learned to read and write before I ever went to school. I didn't play with dolls or toys much. I always wanted a book or to be drawing something. Even as a little kid, I liked books better than toys." She paused for a moment. "I always knew," she said with sudden intensity.

"Knew what?" I asked.

"That I was going to be a teacher. I wanted to help people and I knew that I would be a teacher to do that."

Her words sank into me and I envied her certainty. "You helped me," I said quietly.

"I hope so," she responded with her Mona Lisa smile.

4 – Respect

The next time I visited Mrs. Thomas I had already started the fall semester at Louisiana College in Alexandria. As Director of Criminal Justice, I taught Introduction to Criminal Justice, Criminal Law, Civil Law, and Juvenile Delinquency while working on a committee to set up the law school that was due to open its doors fall semester 2013. When the law school opened in Shreveport, I would become the Director of Academic Success Programs. Because of the two hour distance between the two campuses, I would eventually move to Shreveport.

She was glad to see me when I arrived. Her hair was perfectly coiffed belying her trip to the beauty parlor that morning. Mrs. Thomas was known for her fashion sense and she never appeared in public disarrayed or what others would call casual. She was all business.

"So, how is it going?" she asked, eager to hear about my start at the college. I told her it was going well and that the students seemed interested. My classes were small and it gave me more time with each student. At Kennesaw my classes had been much larger and motivation fluctuated. I remembered my own days as a student when my focus concentrated on one thing – girls, and to be honest, outright laziness. It took a while for me to understand that what I did day in and day out impacted the outcome.

"What makes a good student?" I asked her.

She smiled and laughed within herself. "Well, all kinds of things, I expect. Intelligence, the capacity for hard work, a desire to learn, but I think the thing that matters the most is how you're brought up."

I leaned forward sitting on the sofa placing my elbows on my knees. My hands met and my fingers tapped together in mirrored reflection. I let the thought sink in and I thought of my own parents and their insistence that we all do well in school. As I started to recall being "set down for a talkin' to" and a whipping switch, she continued.

"You know, we were just as poor as everybody else. My mother went to the eighth grade and my father went to the sixth grade. My father's parents were gone and he lived with his sister. They were on their own. She got married when he was 12 and he had no place to go. So, a white man who owned a gasoline station took him in. My father worked for him but the white man didn't send him to school. My father didn't want to go, anyway, because he was so far behind. He could read and write but he wasn't up on his other subjects. When he got his job at Chevron after I was born, he took adult education classes and did very well but he worked hard. My mother, though, she just had a lot of natural wisdom and she would do anything for us.

"In those days it was all about having proper home training. We had rules we had to go by. We had to keep our room clean. You could not talk back to a grown person.

You knew not to say anything ugly to an older person. You could not act ugly at school not even to a school mate.

"Getting an education was number one with my parents but we had to be good, good, good children. 'Good children live longer,' they told us," and she looked up and smiled, "I think they were right.

"They would sit us down and talk to us and tell us what they expected of us, what they wanted us to do, and you know, you just had to do it. They would say, 'If you do this, it's going to hurt me, you know?' So, you just didn't want to do any wrong.

"At every meal we would talk about what we had done that day and we were told, 'Don't misbehave at school.' You had to show that you had good home training and that your parents loved you."

Mrs. Thomas straightened her back, sitting up straight and lifted her finger in the air, taking on her mother's persona. "'Now don't you get out there and act like I haven't taught you anything,' she'd say" as she shook her finger at me. "When she put a finger in your face, you knew she meant business.

"They insisted that you put in your best effort at school. You were to speak proper English. You were not going to go to school, simply wear your clothes, and eat lunch. You had to do some pretty good work and have pretty good grades. You had better be good at school, otherwise, Mr. Lawrence, my daddy, was going to see what was wrong. And, hmmm, everybody would be crying then. He didn't whip us but my mother would tear you up." She shook her head at the memory of her parents' discipline. It was nothing to fool around with.

"Everybody in the house had to get a high school diploma with an option to go to college. Now, some decided not to go to college but they all graduated from high school."

She turned to me suddenly and said, "You know, Fred, it all comes down to respect. My parents showed me the respect that I deserved and taught me to demand that respect from others. To do that I had to respect myself. If you respect yourself and others, everything else should fall into line. Don't you think?"

"Yes," I nodded, "yes, I do." A lot of what she told me about her own parents sounded a lot like my own. In our family everyone played their part. We were expected to work together as a family and as a team. In the field we picked cucumbers, peas, butterbeans, and potatoes together. Dad would say, "If one of you ain't finished with his work, ain't NONE of YOU finished."

A lack of respect for the family was a serious matter. I had gone through a spell of rebellion when I was around sixteen, just about the first time I met Mrs. Thomas. I had a job chopping cotton. Mr. Marlow Higgins drove the hoe-truck for white farmers picking up temporary day workers. I was working in the field, goofing off and he caught me throwing cotton bulbs. He fired me on the spot. I had a long walk home that day and when I told my mother about it, she lit into me. She called Mr. Marlow that evening and pleaded with him to take me back. The next morning she marched me to where he picked up day laborers and told him that she would stand good for my behavior. He took me back and I kept my mother's promise. She had made it clear to me that not only did the family need the money I made, but I was also disrespecting my parents and myself with my errant ways.

When I started high school, integration put us into Winnsboro High School, previously an all-white school. The building was well kept and I got into a work-study program picking up the grounds every morning before school started and monitoring the overall cleanliness of the campus. Our segregated middle school had been the stepchild recipient of the white school system. We got the used desks and textbooks. When I went to high school, I saw the new desks and blackboards and the clean windows and it grated on me. Being a teenager has its own set of problems, but I didn't help myself with a bad attitude. I was constantly getting in trouble running my mouth and smarting off. One of my teachers, Mrs. Ollie Polk, sent me to the office every day one week. In those days, capital punishment consisted of being sent to the principal's office for a pre-determined number of whacks with a paddle depending on the offense. Holes were drilled in the paddle for ultimate sound effect and it was a matter of discussion between students on whether the air whooshing through the holes intensified the pain threshold. I had the undignified distinction of being served the paddle by Mr. Sartin, Mr. Shell, and Mr. Singleton. My older brother, Leroy, stayed in trouble more often than I did and because he had asthma, Mr. Shell would call for my mother to come into school and administer the paddle. For Leroy, that punishment had an additional sting. She may not have been able to smack as hard as Mr. Shell but she certainly had the ability to make Leroy miserable for a longer period of time. Due to my mother's persistence, Leroy and I both finished high school the same year.

It was about that time that I met Mrs. Thomas and she began to teach me about self-respect. "You know, Fred," she said once, "If you play with a puppy, it'll lick your face." I didn't have any idea what she was talking about but the tone of her voice and the look on her face made it clear that I was playing with fire and she wasn't going to tolerate it. It was that day that I began to understand that respect started with yourself.

5 – Determination

Our next visit came with banana pudding and sweet iced tea. Mrs. Thomas had made a large batch of banana pudding for a family gathering and she made up one smaller pan just for my visit. As I spooned it into my mouth, I silently prayed for forgiveness as I forsook my diet. I alternately enjoyed food and did penance by abstaining from it when the scales tipped unfavorably. The conflict when faced with Mrs. Thomas' banana pudding was too much to bear so I decided to enjoy the gift of her cooking.

"You know, cooking is just science and a little math," she said. I looked up at her while licking the spoon clean.

"How's that?" I asked.

"Well, you know, chemical properties that complement other properties in measured quantities under diverse conditions of heat ultimately appeal to the biological trigger of hunger," she smiled, "You just mix some stuff together, cook it, and it's good to eat!" I nodded in agreement while taking another bite.

"Why did you study science?" I asked.

"Well, I intended to take a degree in math because I was such a math whiz in high school," she started, "but when I got to college I met some really disagreeable math teachers, and I decided to change over to biology because

I really loved science, too. The more I got into it, the more I loved it. When Crick and Watson came out with the structure of the DNA molecule, I saw all kinds of applications. The Jarvis heart was another big step. It changed the whole way we looked at cardiovascular disease. Sometimes you think about big advances in science and how they happened in the distant past, but these things happened while I was teaching. Can you believe how exciting that is?" Her face was glowing and I saw the passion of teaching once again.

"There are not a lot of women who go into math or science. It was even more unusual when you were in school, don't you think?" I asked while scraping the bottom of the bowl.

"Yes, that's true. But I don't think I was a lot like the other girls in school. I didn't hang out and do a lot of the silly things girls do together. I would have rather read a book and I was always studying. I wanted to do really well in school and I did," she responded.

"Now, I always wanted to look nice. I learned to sew and once I got a job, I made a dress every day. I wanted my clothes to fit me nicely and I wanted everything to match, so I made my own clothes. Besides, I wasn't tall enough for the clothes that were sold in the stores and I didn't have a lot of money, so it worked out fine," she explained.

"Is sewing a science or a math?" I asked. Her narrowed eyes and pursed lips told me sarcasm wasn't going to be tolerated. I smiled in apology.

"Where did you get your drive to succeed?" I changed the subject.

"My parents really gave that to me," she said, "But I always knew what I wanted to do. I just wanted to go to college and then be a teacher. I didn't even want to get married! I just wanted to be independent and teach.

"When I think back on it, my parents really helped define my ambition. My mother taught me what I know about living but my dad gave me my identity. He used to tell me, 'Baby, I want you to be an independent little lady. I don't want you to have to ask nobody for nothing but if you do, don't be too proud . . . be humble about it.' So, to this day I don't go borrowing from somebody, not even a cup of sugar.

Lillie Lawrence
Mabel Thomas' Mother

"My daddy taught me how to drive when I was twelve or thirteen years old but I never drove until after I was married. We bought a 1964 Mustang when we got married and we still have that car. My daddy loved to go places; he loved adventure. Once, he got a job driving white folks around and he really liked it and the money was pretty good. He drove them all around New Orleans. But then they started going out of town quite a bit and he would stay overnight with them and my mother complained about it. 'Noles,' she said, 'You need to be at home with these children.' So he stopped driving them and he got his job at Chevron and he stayed there until he retired.

Noles Lawrence
Mabel Thomas' Father

"My parents expressed love, concern, and encouragement from day one. They provided for us in every way they possibly could. It may have been on a low level scale, but we had food, clothing, and shelter. Every night we ate dinner together and they discussed guidelines for living. The older siblings had to take care of the younger ones with as much protection, caring, and love as our parents. We had a pecking order but the older ones never chastised us. That was our parents' job.

"I remember when I was about three years old; my mother told me I was going to get a baby brother. I said, 'Now, why are you going to get me a brother? I didn't ask you to give me a brother.'" We both laughed at the scene.

Mabel Thomas' Brothers - Left to Right: Freddy Lawrence, Sr.; Sherman Lawrence, Sr. (back center); Noles Lawrence, Jr. (front center, deceased); James L. Lawrence, Sr.

"But over time," she continued, "I lost a sister and a brother." She pursed her lips and looked away. She was silent for a few moments but then she rallied, "My parents were the most important influence in my life. They taught us to respect other people and to respect ourselves. We were taught that there are good people in the world and bad people. It is our reaction to people that brings out the good or the bad. If you respect people and respect yourself, then people, in turn, will react the same way to you. If you were kind and nice to people, they would be nice to you and that's the way I conducted myself.

Mabel Thomas' Sisters - Left to Right: Mabel L. Thomas; Leah L. Watson (back center); Julia L. Homer (front center, deceased); Lille Rose L. Hill

"When my father worked at Chevron, he became close friends with a white man. In fact, he was well liked by several of the men who worked there because he helped them with all kinds of service jobs. He had a good reputation. This man came to our house and we got to know him. He brought Christmas gifts for the entire family. When I was little, he asked me what I wanted for Christmas and I told him books! He brought me lots of books," she smiled at the memory.

"When I was in high school, I was tested for intelligence and my scores were high enough to be a candidate for MENSA. I was on my way to college. I even got an invitation to attend MIT. My parents didn't know how they were going to pay for it but they were determined to make it work. My father told his friend about my plans for college, but he didn't ask for anything. Do you know that man put money in my father's credit union account every payday to help pay for my college education? Not only that, he went around to the other white men who worked there and they put in money, too.

"After my father retired, he kept in touch with this man and then one day he found out he had died. He wasn't able to go to his funeral because he found out afterwards. But this man, because he liked my father, put money into my college fund right up until I graduated. Can you believe that?"

I thought of people in my own life that had been generous with money, professional encouragement, and friendship. Her voice pulled me back to her story.

"When it was time to go off to college, I was so silly; I didn't want to leave my parents. I really wanted to go to college, but I really didn't want to leave home either. You can't have it both ways, can you?

First Steps at University

"When I did leave home, they reminded me of the life rules they had taught me. My mother told me, 'You are a lady. You act like one. You have good sense. You're going off to college to get a good education so you can take care of yourself. Your father and I expect you to do just that.'

"My father said, 'Whatever you do, don't ever take anything from a man. If you need anything, you ask your daddy. I'm your daddy. Whatever it is you need, I will provide for you.'

"My principles of life that I was taught as a child, I will forever carry them with me. I know all of them are outdated, but I still hold onto those principles. They help me govern my life today," her voice quivered and when she looked at me, her eyes were rimmed with tears.

6 – Relationships

My next visit was on a rainy afternoon. I drove in from a meeting in Shreveport and the windshield wipers were doing overtime. The wind blew water across the flat highway and I fought to keep the car in the lane when big gusts of wind threw the rain both vertically and horizontally. It reminded me of the remnants of a hurricane that made its way into northern Louisiana and beyond. It wasn't only the Gulf coastline that got pummeled. Growing up, we had our share of power outages and raging wind and rain. As I pulled into her driveway, I turned off the motor and listened to the rain punish the roof of the car. Deciding it wasn't going to let up any time soon, I opened the car door, wrapped my jacket around me, and dashed for her front door. She was waiting for me as she opened the door wide for me. I stepped inside and hesitated to shake the rain off my coat onto her carpet.

"Come in," she said, "Let me take that wet coat. I'm surprised you came in this weather."

"It wasn't so bad when I started out," I answered, "But it's blowing pretty bad now."

"Sit down and let me get you some coffee. Don't worry about that couch, I've had it forever. You know Otis told me the other day that I don't throw anything out. He said that I was a hoarder, not as bad as the ones you see on television, but a hoarder all the same. I have to say that I agree with him. I can't seem to throw anything out. Everything I have has some connection to somebody. I just can't give it up. Well, someday my family will have a job on their hands!" she chuckled at the thought of them sorting through all her collections and cupboards.

"How long have you lived here?" I asked her taking the hot coffee from her.

"Well, probably about forty years. We rented a house down on 6th Street, which is Carver Street now, right after we got married and then we bought this house a little while later. We've been married for forty-five years. If I don't kill him, we'll be married fifty years before long," she giggled at the thought.

"How long have you been divorced? It's been a long time, hasn't it? Do you want some cookies with your coffee? I've got some of those Pepperidge Farm cookies. They're good," she declared as she got up to go after the cookies. I didn't know which question to answer first.

"I'm fine. I don't need anything," I answered.

"You'll like them," she insisted, bringing back a few cookies on a small green glass plate, "They're good." I took a cookie and dunked it in my coffee. The thought of my diet crossed my mind and I thought, 'I'm going to have to stop coming here.'

The rain beat against the window making it darker than it really was. "So, how long have you been divorced? Your boys are growing up now, aren't they?" she asked.

"Yes, they are. They're in college now and I've been single for over twenty years."

"My Lord, a nice looking professional man like yourself! I can't believe it. Well, you know, I never wanted to get married," she stated.

"Is that right?" I asked, "I thought you and Mr. Thomas were childhood sweethearts."

"Nothing like it," she said bending her head down to underscore the truth. "I didn't meet Otis until I went to Southern University in Baton Rouge. It wasn't like it was love at first sight. He was entertaining another young woman and I was entertaining another young man, so we just knew each other casually. No, we didn't get to know each other better until we both took teaching jobs here in Winnsboro. Neither one of us had any money so we shared rides to school. The whole first year he didn't say anything that a lady would take offense to. He was very polite. But, look out, the second year he started with his moves and getting a little frisky. We bantered around a bit and started talking. He had a very quiet, calm nature. I thought he was kind of cute. He would smile at me and he had pretty white teeth. He was a good looking old black rascal."

"Uh hmmm," I murmured encouraging her to go on.

"I never wanted to get married. I thought all my life that I wanted to be a teacher and a nun. Getting married wasn't on my agenda. Well, we started to get to know each other and before I knew it, we got engaged. At the time I was living with Elizabeth Miller on Carver Street. It was my birthday and it was raining hard, harder than it is right now. All the streets were flooded so I didn't think we would be going anywhere, so I went back to bed with a book and before long, I was sound asleep.

"I heard Elizabeth knocking on my door saying, 'That old crazy boy is out here.' Elizabeth didn't like Otis all that much and I was half asleep and I said, 'I don't want to see any crazy boy.' And she said, 'Well, he's out here and you're going to see him now.'

"Well, I put on my robe and went out into the living room and Otis was standing there nearly drowned, he was so wet. Elizabeth sat down in a chair to see what he was going to do. Otis gave her a look and she finally left the room. He had bought a ring and he walked through those flooded streets to come over and propose to me on my birthday. He was so sweet. I told him I would think about it. Well, he looked like I had just driven a stake through his heart and he asked me if I would accept his ring. So I said yes, I'll accept your ring. And that's how we got engaged on my birthday, March 29, 1964.

"When I told my parents, they were doubtful. 'Are you sure, Baby?' they asked because I had always told them that I didn't want to get married. All I wanted to do was be a teacher and be independent. But I knew I loved him and if I was going to marry anybody, it would be Otis."

"Where did you get married?" I asked.

"At my parents' church in Oakville, Louisiana. We got married the following year on June 12, 1965. We had a formal wedding even though we didn't have any money. At the time, Otis was taking care of his mother, sister, and brother. His father was in California, but he returned after we married. I was the only one of my siblings to have a formal wedding in my mother and father's church. It was just what my parents wanted.

Bride's Arrival at Oakville Baptist Church

"The people who lived next door to my parents had a little store. They were Italian, the Balamentis. Miss Gladys told my mother not to worry about the wedding cake that she was going to have it made. And my mother said, 'Lord, if this woman doesn't know how to make a cake for black folks' wedding, I'm going to shoot her.'"

I laughed at the thought of an Italian immigrant woman planning a wedding cake for an African-American bride.

"But, listen," Mrs. Thomas went on, "That woman had the most beautiful cake made. She had six layers, usually you have three, and she had six. It was the first time I had ever seen a black bride and groom on the top of the cake, but she had them there. I said, 'Bless her heart, yes indeed. I cannot believe it.' She did the little spiral things with the bride and groom and the bridesmaid and groomsman were looking up at the bride. She had it made for me. Gladys Balamenti did that," she smiled at the memory of the nice white woman who lived next door and took such an interest in her family.

"Some other neighbors, an old lady and old man, provided little finger sandwiches made by a caterer. And these people my daddy worked with, another white couple, Mr. and Mrs. Clausen provided the champagne. We had champagne for weeks at my house. They loved my parents. Mr. Clausen even provided a limo for us."

"Where did you go in the limo?" I asked.

Mabel and Otis Thomas - June 12, 1965

The Bride and Cake

"Just from the house down to the church, maybe a mile, just down the highway. We lived right on the highway and the church was right on the corner of the highway so we didn't have to travel very far," she reached into a drawer and pulled out an envelope with snapshots in them.

"Otis' sister was in the wedding. She was a bridesmaid and she wanted to take some pictures to show them to family in California but we never got them back. A man my daddy worked with was a part-time photographer and someone stole our pictures out of his car. Of course, he was parked in front of a bar while he was inside. These pictures were taken by some friends and family. They're all I have."

Enjoying the Cake

"What was the first thing you bought when you got married?"

"Well, it was furniture and that's a funny story. I told you that we had rented a house on 6th Street. We drove over to Monroe and went to Sears Roebuck to buy furniture. The salesman came up to us and he looked at us like we were little toy people. I couldn't blame him because I was only about four feet tall and Otis wasn't more than four feet eight inches.

"We told him we wanted to buy some furniture for our new house because we were getting married. 'Oh, how nice,' he said, 'y'all are getting married. You look so young.' And then he asked us if we had a job yet. We told him yes and we told him that I was 25 and Otis was 27. Well, he was really surprised.

Newlyweds Otis and Mabel Thomas

"So we picked out a bedroom set and he asked what else we wanted. And I told him I didn't think we could afford anything else. He said, 'Leave it to me. I'm going to set you up on a plan where you can get what you need for your house and you'll have money left over to enjoy your married life.' He was a middle-aged white man and we got a dining room outfit and a living room outfit and a black and white TV. I couldn't believe it. We paid less than $100 a month but I was so anxious to get rid of the debt, I made sure we paid it on time and never missed a payment. I still have all of those things except I gave away the living room outfit after Katrina."

"What was the biggest challenge in your marriage?" I asked hoping that I hadn't asked something too personal.

"Well," she said, "There were a couple of things that nearly brought it all down. We weren't married very long. In fact, it was the following May before our first anniversary, Otis and his friend, Solomon Neal, were going to spend the day together just riding around. They did that every once in a while and I didn't think anything about it.

"That afternoon around 5:30 Otis' brother came over. Solomon and Otis had been in a terrible accident outside of Rayville on their way home. Otis still had his mother's address on his ID and the police had called her. His brother said that he was at St. Francis Hospital in Monroe but for some reason, he couldn't take me over there. So I called Otis' father and he didn't know where the hospital was and he was too upset to take me. Then I called Otis' sister and her husband and they agreed to take me.

"About an hour later they came to pick me up. We drove around Monroe and couldn't find the hospital. When we arrived, I walked in the door and could see him on a stretcher as bloody as he could be. His face was covered with blood. I told the policeman at the door that I wanted to see my husband Otis Thomas. The policeman went in and told the doctor that a young lady was in the hallway and she said her daddy had been in an accident. He asked if this man was Thomas.

"The doctor told him to have me wait a few minutes. I sat in the waiting room with my sister-in-law, her husband, and another woman they had with them. The doctor came out and asked, 'Who's with Thomas?' I raised my hand and he said, 'Do you want to see him? You're not going to be upset or anything?' I said, 'Yes, I do want to see him. I'll try not to be upset. Can he talk?' He said, 'Yes, he can talk. He's a little groggy because we knocked him out. He'll be out in a few minutes.'

"We went into the room and the doctor asked, 'Thomas, do you know who this is?' 'Yeah, yeah,' Otis told him. And the doctor said, 'I'm going to leave you a while to talk with your daughter.' And he said, 'My daughter? That's my wife!' And he said, 'Your wife? Man, you robbed the crib.' He laughed and then left the room.

"I walked up to Otis' bed and took his hand. 'We had an accident,' he said, 'We had an accident.' 'Where's Solomon?' I asked him and he told me he didn't know.

Two policemen came in and said to me, 'Ma'am, if you'll excuse us, I would like to talk with your daddy for a few more minutes.' And I thought, what's this daddy stuff going on?

"The policeman asked Otis, 'Mr. Thomas, can you hear me?'

"'Yes, I can hear you,' Otis said. The policeman asked him what happened and he told him that they just had an accident.

"'What kind of car were you driving?' the policeman asked.

"'I wasn't driving any car. My car is at home. You can ask my wife,' Otis told him.

"'Where's your wife?' the policeman asked, 'Was she in the car with you? Or was she driving?'

"'This is my wife right here,' and Otis lifted his hand in my direction.

"'The policeman turned around and said, 'I'm sorry, Miss, they told me that he was your daddy.'

"'No,' I said, 'this is my husband and his car is at home. He was riding with a friend.'

"The doctor told us that he was going to keep Otis overnight and so my sister-in-law and her husband and their friend left. I was sitting alone in the hospital room with Otis and his head just kept bleeding. I looked at his head and saw how bad he was hurt and I went and asked the nurse to call in a doctor. When the doctor came in he said he could give him something that would stop the bleeding but I had to decide whether to give it to him or not. If we didn't give it to him, he could bleed to death. If we gave him the medicine, it may stop it or he could go into a state of shock and die as a result.

"I just thought, 'What am I going to do about this? I just don't know.' I turned to the doctor and told him, 'I just don't know want to say.'

"And the doctor said, 'Well, it'll be up to you because he definitely can't tell you anything. He can't make a decision and if you decide to give it to him, you'll have to sign for the payment because it's something that the insurance doesn't pay for.'

"I said to myself, 'Lord Jesus, what am I going to do?' I didn't have any money with me. I had picked up a twenty dollar bill from the dresser but I gave it to my sister-in-law's husband for gas to bring me to the hospital. I turned to the doctor and told him I would have to pray about it.

"He said, 'I'll be right down the hall and whenever you get ready, Mrs. Thomas, you may call.'

"I said, 'Yes sir, I will.' I sat there and prayed and asked the good Lord to just give me something, anything to help me make this decision because 'Lord, I just do not know what to do.' I sat there with my eyes closed and a small voice from inside said, 'You better get up before he bleeds to death in the bed.' I called the nurse and told her to call the doctor. He came in right away, 'What did you decide to do, Mrs. Thomas?' And I told him to give him the medicine. I signed the form and told the doctor, 'If I'm not able to pay for this medicine and if he lives, he'll come back and work for you.' The doctor looked at me like I was crazy. He gave him the medicine and the blood stopped just like that. He told me that the nurses would clean him up and wrap his head.

"Before he left, he said, 'Good night, Mrs. Thomas. I hope he sleeps well and that you will, too.' I said, 'Thank you. I hope you will, too.' It was about five o'clock in the morning. About six o'clock that morning the phone rang and I thought it must be Otis' family. When I picked up the phone, I heard my mother say, 'Mabel?' Oh Fred, I just cried. I said, 'Mama? How did you know where I was?' She said she had been calling people like crazy and they told her about the accident and she asked, 'Where is my child?' and they told her that I had gone to Monroe to see about it. She called every hospital in the Monroe area until she finally found one that had an Otis Thomas. She prayed with me over the phone and before she hung up, she said, 'Mabel, you can do whatever is necessary to do. You're able.' 'Yes ma'am,' I told her and hung up the phone.

"I was at St. Francis Hospital for three days and three nights and didn't see another soul that I knew but on the fourth day Ephron Rollings came by and noticed me. He had a family member in the hospital and when he found out I had been there for so long by myself he said he would take me home to get some things and then bring me right back. About that time one of the hospital workers who had been so nice to me said that she would sit with Otis while I was gone. 'I'll be right here to watch over him for you,' she said, 'He'll be all right.'

"Well, he wasn't all right. He had eighteen breaks in his legs and I had to decide on whether to have his legs amputated and bring him home or put him in traction and stay in the hospital. They warned me that he might have a terrible limp if the bones wouldn't mend right. In the one leg he had to have a pin inserted above the knee and one below the knee.

"The doctor told me that he would have to be in the hospital for two months. I told him to do whatever he needed to do to save his leg. I didn't know how we were going to pay for the hospital bills but I told the doctor again that when Otis got better, he would come back and work for the hospital. He just laughed at me. He was pretty used to us by then.

"I finally found out about the accident. Solomon was trying to pass a tractor but he didn't clear it. A white man was driving the tractor and Solomon hit it on Otis' side of the car. Two black men were riding on the back of the tractor and they could see that Solomon wasn't going to clear it, so they jumped off. The white man was in the hospital and I met his wife. She said they couldn't afford for him to stay in the hospital and she was going to take him home and take him to the doctor every day. I saw them again at a court hearing and he looked like an old, old man but he wasn't. He was all broken up, arthritis had set in, and he could barely walk. He died about a month later.

"Well, two months went by and then the doctor said it would be another two to three months. I was frantic about how I was going to handle him and the hospital bills. I met with the billing manager and told her I could handle $100 a month and she prepared a payment book for me. You know how you pay your car off in three years? Well, I had five years to pay the hospital. I prayed, 'Lord, if you make a way for me, I'm going to make sure that I pay these people every penny that I owe.'

"One day another man came in to share Otis' room. I had been sleeping on the extra bed whenever I needed to rest. This man had been to the dentist and the doctor found a tumor behind his teeth. They brought him in to remove the tumor and half his face was gone. I closed the curtain between his and Otis' beds to give us some privacy and a little while later, I heard him coughing. Then I heard him sneeze and I saw splatters of blood all over his side of the curtain. I opened the curtain and he had blown the dressing right off his face and his entire head was a bloody mess. I ran to get the nurses. While they were working on him, his wife came in, took one look, turned around and left. I didn't think he would make it.

"They released him from the hospital a couple of days later and I thought we would never see him again. Well, two weeks later, he came strolling back into the hospital to see Otis. He was fine!

"Otis stayed in the hospital for another two months before he finally came home. He still needed to be in a body cast so I had to get a hospital bed with a trapeze bar so he could lift himself. But his feet did not touch the floor for six solid months. I had to go back to work four days after we got home from the hospital and I didn't know what I was going to do. That's when God sends angels and he sent our neighbor across the street, Gus Spencer. Mr. Spencer came every day and gave Otis the lunch I had left in the refrigerator and stayed with him until I got home in the afternoon. He did that for three months and never took a penny for his trouble.

7 – Prejudice

My time was spent between Winnsboro, Baton Rouge, and Shreveport in a rotating panorama of family events, teaching classes, and committee meetings for the Judge Paul Pressler School of Law. I was busy and yet still trying to find a niche where my routine met my comfort zone. I knew it would come but it just wasn't coming soon enough.

On my way back into Winnsboro I passed by the ball field where I had played baseball with my friends. There were two ball fields, not because there were multiple leagues in Winnsboro but because before integration, there was a field for white players and one for black players. Even today, Winnsboro is a friendly town but community lines are clearly drawn. I drove by the ice cream stand that had closed a long time ago. Weeds sprouted around it but I saw myself as a young boy standing on one side to be served in the colored line. White customers were served on the other side. I remembered reading about the Freedom Riders during the struggle for integration. Mixed groups of black and white men and women rode Trailways and Greyhound buses on different routes throughout the south. They staged the bus to quietly challenge the segregation pattern. White men would sit in the back while black women would sit up front. Sometimes a black man and a white woman would sit together. When a bus stopped at roadside restaurants, they would cross service lines with a white patron sitting in the section for black customers or a black person would drink from a whites only drinking fountain. It seems tame enough today but back then people were beaten or worse for a non-violent plea for equality.

I pulled into a parking spot in front of the drug store and looked across the street at the movie theater. I had been there many times as a boy when blacks sat in the balcony and whites on the main floor. One day I went to see *Smokey and the Bandit* and I casually went in and sat in a seat on the main floor. About five or ten minutes after the movie started, the police walked in and beckoned me to come with them. I followed them out of the theater and I was asked to leave, so I did.

As a teenage boy, these things gnawed at me and I was building an internal fire fueled by anger. As a very young man I was learning to hate white men. I started hanging out with a group of boys that brought out the worst in me. I was frustrated because I wasn't making the grades I should have been making and some of my other friends were doing better in school than I was. I knew I had to do better but I didn't know how to turn it around. Then I took a biology class. I was sixteen years old and I walked into Mrs. Thomas' class and then I began to learn more than biology.

I had earned the reputation as a trouble maker and I was certainly sent to the principal's office enough times but Mrs. Thomas acted like she didn't know any of it. She smiled at me every time I came to class and seemed to take a special interest in me. I didn't buy it right away – I was too cool to let a little short woman try to teach me anything. So I started acting out in her class and smarting off. One day she walked up to me and my friends and said in a firm tone, "Fred Jones, you're an embarrassment to the Jones family name." I was stunned by her boldness and ashamed of the truth of her statement. From then on I decided I would be different and I would be better than I was then.

I began to watch her and how she acted. She had a passion for teaching and she actually liked her students. She knew how to bring out the best in her students, at least the ones who cared to have dreams.

"What do you want to do with your life?" she asked me one day.

"I want to be a lawyer," I replied.

"Then be one and be a good one," she challenged.

During class, she would throw out little wisdoms and I started to write them down in the back of my notebook. They began to change the way I looked at life:

Young Teacher

- There are going to be good days and bad days. Happy and sad days. There'll be times when people will give you a hard time and you have to suffer the consequences.
- You should reach out to someone somewhere along in life so you can say, 'I tried to help somebody along the way.'

- We're all unique and that is a gift from God.

- We know we cannot move mountains and we can't change the heart of man or the minds of many people. We can help them along the way but it's up to the individual to do what is necessary for them.

- Some people don't have real dreams or goals. They fantasize. They think of things but they're not really trying to accomplish them. We limit ourselves when we don't face reality.

- Your attitude comes from what you're taught when you're a baby because I don't think you're born with hatred or dislike for people.

- A lot of black people have been taught that they are less than whites. When you begin to think like that, you're putting a limitation on yourself because you're holding yourself back. You'll be too afraid, angry, or disgusted to really function to your full extent. You've limited yourself right there.

- Encouragement is very important. Encourage others.

- If we could just look at people as people just like we look at cats and dogs as cats and dogs or chickens as chickens and birds as birds, then I think it would be a wonderful world.

- Regardless of what color you are, what nationality you are, or what ethnic group you belong to, or what religious group you belong to, we're people. We're people because of what's inside of our hearts.

- I'm who I am because I'm me. The good Lord made me. I don't think he decided, 'Well, you're going to have to be this color, little black girl.'

- There shouldn't be any barrier or hatred or animosity because of color or ethnicity or religion. I think that is the primary problem in the world today. I think it is because we judge others based on those kinds of things.

- Discipline yourself.

- You must learn people, learn how to be positive about things, have positive outlooks. Don't always look at things negatively or come up with an excuse. If you start giving excuses, you'll find that you lose the real world because you drop out from reality.

- Stay real and be yourself. Know that who you are lies in your heart and not in your mouth or in your pocketbook.

Once I tried to explain to her about how I felt about racial inequities. "You know that private all white school, Franklin Academy?"

"Yes," she replied.

"I've never even stepped on the grounds," I spat out.

"So, what's that to you?" she asked calmly.

"They're discriminating against us!" I accused.

"Then that's their problem, isn't it?" she replied, "Are you going to let it be your problem, too?"

8 – Love

When I pulled into the driveway, I could see her cutting roses in her back yard. Her face broke into a broad smile as I approached her and she held up her fresh cuttings, "I've been playing in the dirt!"

"I see that," I said moving closer to examine the quality of the flowers, "They're beautiful."

"Yes, they are. But they need a lot of attention. The deer like them for one thing but they haven't been around much lately. Do you know that the Latin name for rose is rosa? Sounds Spanish and hardly worth the effort. I would think it would sound more Latin, like rosanthium" she mused as she cut off a dead flower from her bush.

"Did you study botany in your sciences?" I asked her.

"No, not really. Just an overview. Plants are their own mystery. Did you know that the color of a rose means different things – like a red rose means passion or love? Given anyone red roses lately?" she teased.

"No," I blushed and shook my head, "Not for a long time. I only give roses to my favorite teachers."

She shook her head at the ambitious compliment and handed me a rose, "My oldest brother used to give me red roses every birthday. I can't think of anything I loved more. They were beautiful."

"Doesn't Mr. Thomas give you roses?" I asked.

"No," she shook her head, "Otis is just laid back and really doesn't show his emotions. I would be worried if he did give me roses." She laughed. Her face became serious and she looked me in the face.

"Were you happy when you were married?" she asked.

"Yes, for a while," I admitted, "But then we were young and we didn't know how to make it work any longer."

"I know," she agreed, "You can lose your way when you're young. Sometimes even when you're not so young." She bent over to cut another rose and asked, "Don't you have two sons?"

"Yes, I do," I responded reaching for my wallet to show her their picture, "Jonathan is in Tyler at the University of Texas studying psychology and Freddie is still up in Atlanta working and trying to go to school. They're as different as day and night. I never could understand how two kids in the same family could be so different."

"No," she said, "I'm real different than my brothers and sisters. Of course, they think I'm the oddball and they're probably right."

"You and Mr. Thomas never had any children, did you?" I probed gently.

"No, I never wanted any children. I prayed all the time, 'Lord, I love my husband but please don't give me any children,'" she gestured wildly like nothing worse could happen.

"Don't get me wrong," she said, "I love kids and I love my students but I wanted my own private independence. I know what a tough job it is to have kids. You know, because I was younger in my family, my older sisters and brother had kids and I was always doing laundry and taking care of kids. I knew I didn't want any of my own. But as it wound up, we had three girls that God brought our way."

She sat down in the metal outdoor chair and I took the one next to her. "They weren't my children, of course, but I call them my children of love. They just came out of the blue."

"How is that?" I asked, confused.

"Well, you know Stephanie and I think you remember Kim. You may have met Sonja. Maybe not. They came to us differently as if God was opening a door that let them in, one by one. Sometimes they came with joy and sometimes with a little pain mixed in. But, in the end, I wouldn't have had it any other way.

"Sonja was my niece, my sister Lillie Rose's daughter. Sonja LaNeka Hill – what a beautiful child! Ever since she was two years old, she came to stay with me every summer until she was 17 years old. That girl was the light of my life. Hmmm – she was the sweetest thing. So generous, so thoughtful. She would buy me little gifts for my birthday and holidays.

"When she graduated from high school, she went to Southern University in Baton Rouge and in New Orleans where she lived. She became a teacher – I wonder where she got that idea! – and taught for seven years. When Katrina came, she was part of the evacuation, and she came to live in Winnsboro with us. She died of complications from diabetes two years later. It was on May 24, 2007, one of the saddest days of my life. I don't think I'm over it still. But she had a little girl and she's as sweet as Sonja was. We see quite a bit of her and I admit that I spoil her. You know, she's one of my grandchildren now, Morgan Hill is her name. Sonja never married but she lived as full a life as she could. She simply embraced life. "

Niece Sonja LaNeka Hill

"What about Stephanie?" I didn't know the whole story and I felt a little like I was prying into her personal life but she seemed like she wanted to tell me.

She sighed and began, "Stephanie came into our lives when she was in the 9th grade at Winnsboro High. I was teaching biology, of course, and we were discussing genetics and I told the students that the only thing that was different from man and all of the other animals is that man had the intelligence to know who his parents were. I told them that their little cousins the apes, orangutans, and chimpanzees know who their parents are too but they don't take to them like our parents take to us.

"Now, I remember Stephanie just looking at me and I went on, 'There's one right that every person should have and that is to know who their biological parents are.' One of the kids asked, 'Well, Mrs. Thomas, suppose you're adopted?'

"I said, 'Whoever you're living with or whoever is feeding you or clothing you, you can consider them as your parents. But, your biological parents, through whatever means, you may never need them. But you do have parents. People you love, right?'

"'Yes, ma'am.'

"So Stephanie came up to me after class and she said, 'Are you sure everybody ought to know who their own parents are?'

"And I said, 'Oh, by all means I think so, darling.'

"'But how do you find out?' she asked.

"Well, DNA can help you find out and you can always talk to your mom or dad or whoever you're with, a grandparent. They might know and they may tell you.' She still looked confused so I said, 'That's something they should tell you.'

"Later on I had hall duty with Mrs. Brass and Stephanie walked past. I said to Brassie, 'You know, that girl looks like somebody I know.' Brassie started to laugh and gave me a look that I didn't understand at the time and said, 'Well, you might know her.'

"Stephanie was in the Science Club and she was in my class the next year. She was smart, had a good mind. The first day of school she came in and sat on my desk and talked and talked and talked. She knew that the Science Club was going to Hot Springs, Arkansas that year and she asked, 'Can I go, too?'

"'Sure,' I said, 'you're a member of the Science Club so you're eligible to go.'

"'My mother wants you to call her because she doesn't want me to be a problem for you. She's afraid I won't behave,' she ducked her head down and looked at me sideways.

"So I called her mother and told her that she was going to be in my care and she knew how strict I was and she would be fine. When we got to Hot Springs, Stephanie came to me and asked if she could sleep in my room. I told her she needed to sleep with Lisa in the room they were assigned. She didn't want to sleep with the other girls, so finally I told her she could sleep on the extra bed in my room. She sat on the bed and talked late into the night and the more she talked, the more I looked at her face. Her smile was so familiar, and you won't believe this, Fred, but she smelled like Otis."

"She smelled like Otis?" I asked incredulous.

"Yes, I know it sounds odd but her body chemistry made her smell like Otis. I can't explain it but it began to dawn on me that this child was more than just another student. She finally fell asleep and I watched her for a while. I began to put it together, her need for my attention, the way she didn't seem to belong to her own family, her smile and yes, even the smell. Never in my whole life would I have thought that my husband would be unfaithful to me especially after I nursed him back to health after the accident. I was incredibly hurt and then the anger began to surge.

"When we got home, I confronted him and he denied it all. I screamed at him in absolute blind fury and he still denied it. Finally, I told him to pack his things and get out. He still begged me to believe him. 'All I want is the truth,' I told him and that's when he admitted it. He said he didn't know Stephanie's mother even had a baby until she was several years old. He was crying; I was crying. It was horrible.

"I went to visit my mother a few days after that. Otis didn't want me to go. He was afraid I wouldn't come back. I sat in her kitchen for three solid days crying. I went on and on about how I could have accepted any job I wanted if I hadn't been married to him. I could have gone to Texas, Minnesota, or Chicago. I could have gone to graduate school and gotten my Ph.D. by now if it weren't for him. I ranted on and on and she just sat there listening.

"On the third day, she sat across the kitchen table and asked, 'Are you done crying, now?'

"'Yes, ma'am,' I said because I was all cried out.

"'Then listen to me,' she said, 'Mabel, you know what you're capable of doing. You know what you want in life and it's up to you to set your own goals and make up your own mind on what you want to achieve. You've worked hard, God knows, but Baby, you need to apply that same strength to living your life. If you want to leave Otis, then do it, and don't look back.'

"I looked up at her because I never thought she would say something like that.

"'But this man is sorry, very sorry for what he's done. I don't doubt for a minute that he loves you. But it has to be your choice to go back to him. And if you decide to go back to him, there's going to have to be forgiveness, there's going to have to be recommitment, and there's going to have to be love.'

"I started to cry again because the pain was so great and I didn't know if I had it in me to start over again.

"'Your father and I are coming up to our 50th wedding anniversary soon. If you decide to go back to him, I want you to promise that you'll try for your 50th, too. I've challenged your sisters and brothers with the same promise, but, Baby, marriage is for life and you have to work as hard on it as you have on all your other achievements. It needs to be your focus.'

"I started crying again. I don't know where all that water was coming from but I was bawling like nobody's business.

"'There's one more thing,' Mama said, 'There's a little girl who's looking for answers. What are you going to do about that?'

"I packed up my bag and started the drive back to Winnsboro. Even then I wasn't sure I wanted Otis back but in my mind I saw his face pleading with me. I remembered the puddles his wet clothes made when he kneeled down to propose to me. I remembered the times when I was overwhelmed and overworked and he held me in his arms in his quiet embrace. For all my frenetic activity, he was my safe harbor. His calmness evened out my busyness and gave me a place to rest. I would lose more than an unfaithful husband if I walked away now.

"By the time I got to Winnsboro, I was drained of anger and hurt. I was just an empty vessel feeling nothing, waiting for I don't know what. Otis didn't know what to expect when I got home and he was very, very careful. He treated me like a little china doll that might just break into a million pieces. We talked all afternoon and most of the night. At the end, we held on to each other like a tidal wave was going to sweep us away. We decided to take it one day at a time. After about a month, I suggested that if her mother was willing, Stephanie should come live with us.

"I'll never forget the day that child got out of the car with Otis carrying her suitcase. She ran up to me and held onto me like she had been missing me all of her life. That day, she became my daughter, too."

She picked up a photograph of two young women sitting side by side, "That's Stephanie on the left. She's very reserved and serious but really she has a kind heart. She got married while she was in college but she's divorced now. She has three boys – Damone, Jermaine, and Otis – there always has to be an Otis, doesn't there?" she laughed. "Wesby is their family name, Damone, Jermaine, and Otis Wesby. Stephanie went back to her maiden name, Foy. They're rascals, those boys. Lord, have mercy!"

She paused for a moment and pointed to the young woman sitting on the right in the photograph. Thumping the image with her right index finger, she said, "That's Kim. Her given name is Kimona. Pretty, don't you think?"

I nodded and didn't say a word. This was another story that was an honor for her to share and I kept still waiting quietly.

"Kim lived right down the street and when she was about four, she would walk up to my house and just sit and talk with me. She was always in and out, talking, having cookies or Kool-Aid, whatever kids did. She lived with her mother and father. Their name was Authur. Nothing was ever said about Kim and no demands were ever made. When Kim was old enough to go to high school, she was in one of my classes.

"One day she came by the house and asked if she could speak to Mr. Thomas. I told her he wasn't home but was there something I could do for her. She was kind of reluctant to tell me but she finally told me what she wanted. She was about to graduate from high school and she needed some financial help for her graduation. Well, if lightening doesn't strike twice in the same place, then I don't know what to think. I looked into that sweet child's face and saw the whole story.

"When Otis got home, I was sewing, and I asked him, 'Don't you have something to tell me?' When I told him about Kim, he sat down hard, shaking his head like his world was coming to an end. I thought he was going to cry or die right on the spot. I was so mad at him I told him I was going to leave. I knew I wasn't going to leave but I just felt like torturing him. Once I admitted it to myself, I realized I had suspected it for a long time.

"Well, he cried and begged, and I was so sick of it, I just told him that the matter was between him and God and that he would have to deal with it. From that moment on, I put the whole thing in God's hands and I went back to sewing.

"Both Kim and Stephanie went to college and for a while they worked for the same company until it downsized. Kim transferred within the company to another location in Baton Rouge but Stephanie decided to work in the nursing field in Winnsboro.

"Kim has done very well for herself. She's married to Sharvin Guillory and they have two children, Jacob and Joi. I'm so proud of her and of Stephanie, too. They grew up to be independent young women, went to college, and have careers and beautiful children."

She put the picture back in its place and with her back still turned to me, she said, "You know, Fred, I begged God not to give me any children. I really didn't want to be a mother. But he brought me Sonja, Stephanie, and Kim and now these grandchildren. And even though I was so hurt over Otis, I grew as a person because of it and I love him as he is now, not as what I wanted him to be. Love is a tremendous power, Fred. It really can overcome anything. I guess that's why the Bible says that God is love. Don't you think?"

Daughters Stephanie Foy Wesby and Kimona Authur Guillory

I found myself nodding at her and looked into a face that overcame disappointment, betrayal, and anger replacing it with love. Could I be like that?

Otis and Mabel Thomas

9 – Commitment

"Wait until you taste this," she said, "I just made it this morning." She handed me a glass of iced tea and a large slice of coconut cream cake. I looked at it and chastised myself, 'Hmm, hmm, you have no self control whatsoever.' My mission this afternoon included a request for her help. Some of her former students and I were organizing a homecoming appreciation banquet for Mrs. Thomas, Mrs. Mordessa Corbin, and some other teachers. Mrs. Thomas was a treasure-trove of information of people both lost and found. She would help me find the teachers I had lost touch with.

Mrs. Corbin was another one of my favorite teachers. I had worked diligently to get out of the "C" group and I had my sights set on becoming a member of the Beta Club. Betas had to have a B average or better and my report card was teetering on the brink, literally fractions from a solid 3.0. Mrs. Corbin and Mrs. Thomas met and made it possible for me to become a member of the Beta Club. I soared with excitement and I remained a Beta until graduation.

"How did you keep up with all these teachers and students?" I asked her.

"Well, you know me. I don't do anything half way," she wagged her finger at me. "I keep a running list of people's addresses, birthdays, anniversaries. Lord, you should see my Christmas card list. And to tell the truth, a lot of them keep in touch with me.

"Part of it is being involved in the community and in the church. I taught catechism and serve as lector at St. Mary's; sometimes I help Otis with things he's involved in over at First Zion; I've been President of The Black Heritage Organization for twenty years; I work with the Franklin Parish Retired Teachers Association; I help out with the Louisiana Retired Teachers Association sometimes; and there's always something going on with the family. Being involved isn't hard – you just have to show up!"

We laughed because I knew that her energy and vivid interest in the world around her kept her naturally engaged with people. "What makes you become so involved?" I asked her, "Plenty of people show up but they don't participate. You know that from teaching."

Mabel and Otis Thomas
Black Heritage Organization

"Yes, I know," she said, "That was one of the saddest things I encountered. Young people who didn't care about their lives and were just drifting along. It's a perpetual motion thing. You show up for class or an event. You show interest even if you don't want to. You try it even if you don't want to. You master it even if you don't want to. And before you know it, you're an active participant and excelling in spite of yourself. But it starts with just showing up. You have to show up – for work, for class, for life! "

She realized she was on a soapbox and backed off a bit. "It's about commitment, really. You decide what kind of person you want to be and your actions are dictated by that image of yourself. You don't love someone if you're not committed to that person. You don't graduate from college unless you're committed to the process. You don't get promoted in your job unless you're committed to doing well. Commitment is a component of love. Love for yourself and love for others."

I nodded knowing exactly where she stood on commitment. I had seen it in her time and time again. She taught me how to be committed by her example.

"I believe in keeping my word. If I say I'm going to do it, I'm going to do it. Otis thinks that sometimes I do too much but if there is something that someone asks me to do in the community, I'm willing to do it if I can.

"When I was in school I never missed a day of high school. I had perfect attendance. I was valedictorian of my graduating class. Right after final exams and before graduation, we had senior week. We didn't have classes but we had graduation parties and teas. I was never sick but that week, I got the measles, mumps and started my menstrual cycle. I had all kinds of changes taking place. My jaws were so tight I could hardly open my mouth.

"So I woke up on Monday morning with all of these illnesses and my mother took me to the doctor. Well, he confirmed that I had the measles and mumps and told me to go to bed for the next seven days. Oh no, I said, no can do! He wanted to know what I meant and so I told him that I was valedictorian of my class and I had to go to graduation Friday evening and I had to give my speech.

"So he said, 'I don't think you will be able to do it, young lady.'

"'Well, I am,' I said, 'what's going to stop me?' He warned me that the mumps can be hard. He told me that I would spread measles to other people and that once the mumps came into full bloom, I was going to have a hard time opening my mouth to eat.

"I told him, 'By Friday, I'll be ready.' My dad was very concerned and went to the school and talked to the principal, Mrs. Lawrence. She wasn't a relative but she was very understanding and said she would see how things worked out.

"Friday morning I got up and told my mother, 'I'm ready!' She wasn't so sure but I got dressed and went to graduation. My jaws hurt so much and they were so tight but I just prayed, had a swallow of water, and gave my speech. When I was done, I couldn't open my mouth. But I was determined to do it, no matter what, and I did.

High School Graduation

"If I have talent, intelligence, education, and persistence, I think my strongest quality is persistence. I want to do things. And I think persistence has made me get up and do things when I may not want to do them. If you know what your responsibilities are, persistence is what gets them done.

"We all have five senses and you know what you should do and shouldn't do. Persistence, or you can call it commitment, has been the thing that pushed me to do the right thing through the years. Time and time again, persistence of good habits has brought me success.

"The good Lord has enabled me to get an education, and if I have any true talent, then I haven't been able to learn what that is. But intelligence comes from observation, experimentation, and actually studying things. But what good is it all if you're not persistent?" she asked, her head cocked to one side.

I sat there completely absorbed in her words and I had no answer for her convincing persistent argument.

10 – Faith

We were driving down to Monroe together to have lunch at the Waterfront Grill, the site we had chosen for our upcoming Celebrate Teaching banquet. We passed First Zion Baptist Church and Mrs. Thomas pointed it out to me, "That's where Otis goes to church. He's on the Usher Board there."

"Don't you go to church there, too?" I asked.

"No," she said, "I go to St. Mary's Catholic Church. I'm a lector during Sunday mass and I taught catechism. No, I'm a Catholic."

"Is that a problem with Mr. Thomas, the two of you going to different churches?" I didn't mean to pry but it slipped out before I could stop myself.

"It was when I was younger. In those days the Catholic Church didn't tolerate mixed marriages, Catholic and Protestant, but it's different now, more open. I've always gone to the Catholic Church. My mother had me baptized when I was born at Charity Hospital in New Orleans. I get up every Sunday morning and go to Mass . . . rain, sleet, snow, cold, hot, or sick, I am going to church. I tell my husband that I have to pay my respect to God."

"What makes your faith so strong?" I was willing to learn here, too.

"Well, when I was a little girl, I wanted to be a nun. I wanted to take my vows and then be a teacher in a Catholic school. I didn't know it at the time but God had a different plan for me. My faith in God really deepened during a life crisis. I think that's the way it happens with most people. Something happens that's out of your control and then you have no one to turn to but God. He hears us in our weakness, you know. And I think that's when we hear him, too."

I nodded in agreement. I had had the same experience several times.

"I was always so attached to my parents. I adored them and they lavished so much love on me that in some ways, I was more committed to them than I was my husband. One time we were going to New Orleans for the holidays and I called my mother to tell her when to expect us. She said, 'You know, your daddy is in the hospital. He had gall bladder surgery.' And I said, 'Oh, mama. You're kidding.' And she said, 'No, but if you would like to stop by, he would be glad to see you.'

"Well, there was nothing to do but go straight to the hospital when we got into New Orleans. He was asleep when we got there. He hadn't shaven and he had little hairs all over his face. He didn't look like my daddy at all. I called him, 'Daddy?' And he said, 'Oh, Baby! Is that you?' I told Otis right then and there to go on to the house, that I was going to stay the night with my daddy.

"I sat down in the chair next to his bed and I was so tired, I fell right asleep. The next morning I woke up and my dad was up, shaved and dressed and said the doctor had already come, and he was ready to go home. He looked completely different. I called Otis and when he came to pick us up, he said, 'Lord, have mercy, your dad looks like he really has improved.' And I said, 'Yes indeed, he does.' That's the only time I can remember my daddy ever being sick. Now my mother had all kinds of health problems with high blood pressure, diabetes, arthritis, and a malfunctioning kidney, but my daddy was never sick. He went to work every day of his life.

"When I lost my parents in the early 80s, it was a real turning point in my life. They were the most important things in my life. When I was younger, I used to pray and ask the good Lord all the time to please if somebody had to die, let it be me because I didn't think that I would be able to live through the death of my parents. That's the way I always felt. My daddy would always say that children are not supposed to die before their parents.

"When my daddy died, I just lost my identity. I just didn't know who I was and my mind just seemed to have gone blank. Oh, I was still going through the motions but it just wasn't the same. It took some time to get myself together and I really had to do some praying. I talked with my mother every day and she would tell me, 'You have got to let your dad go.' I went home to New Orleans just about every weekend. As soon as I could get away, I went down and spent about two weeks with her.

"She just talked and talked and she told me, 'Now, I don't know what's wrong with you. Why are you that way?'

"I said, 'I don't know. I just miss my daddy.'

"And she said, 'Well look, you know, not just your daddy has died. Someday your mama is going to die too, what are you going to do then?'

"I just cried and she said, 'Baby, I'm so disappointed in you.'

"'Why?' I asked her. 'Fred, that broke my heart.'

"'You don't understand life,' she said.

"'I don't want you to leave mama.' She told me that we're born to die. And when you die, if you live your life right, you go to heaven and be with the Lord. What more can you ask for?

"I prayed about it and I began to see my faith in a bigger dimension. It wasn't just right here, right now; it was for always. My mother's explanation made everything clear about the way life is. It was a turning point in my life. My faith grew tremendously after that. As long as I try and do as the Lord wants me to do, then that's what I'll try and do. Live life every day as it comes.

"I trust in God first and foremost. I trust and depend on the good Lord because faith in God is the greatest power! But faith in yourself is also great. If you have confidence in yourself, regardless of the obstacle, if you just take time to sit down and communicate with God, listen to what he says and have a clean heart – not envious, begrudging, or mean spirited – I think you can face anything.

"I feel that he gives you the strength and the courage to do whatever you have to do. As long as you feel satisfied with yourself and your accomplishments, with who you are and what you're doing, and that you feel as though you're trying to do the Lord's will, then I think that's the greatest accomplishment.

"You must have faith in God. If you don't have faith in God, you'll have a hard time trying to understand who we are and what's going on in the world. If you have a strong faith in God, you'll know that there's a divine being who created order in life. Don't you think so, Fred?"

"Yes," I said, "most definitely."

11 – Self-Awareness

The late afternoon sun alternately lit up her living room and dimmed it. I was setting up a Facebook account for her and explaining about social networking. "See, you log on here and then there's your Wall that people can post things on," I told her.

"What's a Wall?" she wanted to know.

"Kind of like a bulletin board. Your friends can write things on it or put a picture on it and then everyone can see it and comment on it."

"How will my friends know to do that?"

"They'll have a Facebook account too and you can ask to be their friend and when they confirm your request, then you'll be linked together so you can see their Walls and they can see your Wall. You build your social network one friend at a time."

So the only difference in doing this and the usual way you keep in touch with people is that it's done through the computer," she stated.

"Right, but it's faster and you can connect with people from all over at the same time," I explained.

"Why would you want to do that?" she asked.

"To let people know what's going on in your life," I tried, realizing I was trying too hard to sell the concept.

"Sounds like a waste of time," she said. I had to admit that I had often thought the same thing.

"Think of it as a teaching tool," I coached. Her eyes lit up with recognition and suddenly she could see the application. "Here, look at my Facebook page. I have a whole section on the Supreme Court case that my uncle is involved in. See, right here, Otis McDonald v. City of Chicago. I've posted some pictures and comments on everything that happened."

I clicked on a picture of my uncle, Otis, with his attorney and myself, "This was taken on the day of the oral arguments. I was admitted to the United States Supreme Court Bar that day."

"The Supreme Court," she looked at me with wonder, "What was that like?"

"It was the greatest day of my life. When my name was called in open court, I thought I was going to take off like a rocket. And then, when the Justices called my uncle's case, I thought, 'WOW! What is going on here?' I couldn't believe it." My excitement radiated across the table and her face captured it.

"I'm getting carried away," I said.

"Go on," she said, "Get carried away. That's what it's all about."

She pointed at the computer screen, "Will I be able to put things on Facebook like that?" I nodded.

"And Stephanie and the boys will see it?"

"Yes, absolutely," I responded, "And they can add to it. I think you'll like it. It'll be fun." At last, she seemed enthused. I went on to explain that she could keep in touch with her former students, her church friends, and her grandchildren.

"Who will put the pictures on it?" she asked. I began to see myself making several visits and assured her that she would always have help with it.

"I don't like computers much," she sighed, "but I guess they're not going away so we might as well learn to use them."

"That's exactly right. You can do it. You've always conquered everything else," I smiled at her. Conquering challenges was part of her base nature. She gave me a sideways look that said, "Don't you be smart about this."

"Tell me something," she asked, "When you look in the mirror now, what do you see?"

"I see hope," I responded thoughtfully. "I see a boy that you helped get through a rough time and helped turn his life around. I see a young man in law school. I see the first and only black law clerk for a white judge in the 19th Judicial Court in East Baton Rouge Parish. I see a father. I see a minister. I see a teacher," and then I threw my head back and shook my shoulders like a big shot, "And I see a member of the Supreme Court Bar!" We both exploded with laughter until tears rolled down our cheeks. When our laughter subsided, it was my turn to ask.

"Now, you tell me something," I asked, "When you look in the mirror, what do you see?"

She took a few moments to respond, "I thank God that when I look in the mirror, I see a pretty older lady and I feel good about that. I feel good about who I see in the mirror. I don't have any shame or guilt. I am a person who feels good about herself and what she's done in life. My mother and dad used to always tell me, 'Baby, you're a pretty little girl.' I love myself and I feel as though I can stand in front of the Master and say, 'Here I am, Lord.'" She looked at me to see if I doubted her. I didn't.

"I look forward to every birthday. Every year I'm here I have to celebrate. I must be here for some good reason. I look forward to all of my birthdays. Now, of course, I don't look for a big celebration. I'm not that type of person, but I do enjoy getting gifts. No, I don't regret looking forward to another birthday, but I do find that as you get older, some things are not as easy as they used to be. Your steps are a little slower, all the print in things you read is too small, you forget why you came into a room, you know, that kind of thing but all in all, it's not so bad. I have nothing to be afraid of. I know that every day that I live is a blessing from God. No, I really don't have any problems with growing older."

She sat there perfectly dressed, with her hair perfectly done, and her nails perfectly manicured. I couldn't remember the last time I was in conversation with a woman so well put together. Aging just intensified her presence if that was possible.

"What's the best thing about getting older?" I knew I was asking this of a person who didn't seem to have any confidence issues whatsoever.

"Actually," she began, "it's an abundance of freedom. I think the best thing is that you can make all your decisions, right or wrong, without consulting anyone else. My husband can't tell me what to do – not at this age. I only have to keep my principles and God in my life and live how I think the Lord wants me to."

"What's the most important thing in a person's life, do you think?" I felt like I was sitting at the feet of a Greek philosopher.

"I think a person's character, their personality, and their attitude. Those are the things that are important in life. Your character means a lot and the type of lifestyle you live is very important. They're all preparation for how you respond to things in life. A lot of people don't realize that. Suppose someone comes into a large amount of money and it goes to their head. They're going to drive the best cars or live in the best house. But when it comes right down to it, a car is just transportation and a house is just a place to eat and sleep in no matter how big it is. These people think they're moving a step ahead of everybody else and they think they're better or greater, but that's not life. You can't enjoy life like that when you're always looking back to see who got this and who got that and you've got to top it. Life is much more basic than possessions or social status. You have to lay a solid foundation in principles, faith, and who you are."

The sun was starting to set and I looked around at her living room full of pictures, books, and mementos. It was the room of a person connected to others. "What do you like to do?"

"I love reading. I read just about any type of book. I like cookbooks, but I may not follow the recipe. I love sewing, cross stitching, embroidering, and knitting. I made a cross stitch picture for my mother for Mother's Day. She was so thrilled about it, she didn't know what to say. I like to do community work with my church, the Louisiana Retired Teachers Association, and the Black Heritage Association.

You know, I just love the freedom of being retired and not tied to a job and responsibilities. The thing I miss most is the conversations I used to have with my co-workers. But I have friends of all ages, sizes, and color. I love to talk with them especially on an intellectual level. I can't stand idle talk and gossip, never have."

"What's the most important thing you can give another person?" I leaned in to hear her response.

"Well, it's not love, though everyone needs that," she replied, "I think it's respect. Everybody needs to be respected. I've always tried to be a fair person and treat everybody the same way, but my tolerance level is a little shallow when it comes to people who are disrespectful and don't respect themselves."

"Rosa Parks comes to mind and her seat on the bus," I said.

Rosa Parks
www.educationforjustice.org

"Yes, that little woman challenged everyone with her actions, but you know, I don't think at the time that she realized what an impact she was going to have on our whole society. One little woman, sitting on a bus refusing to give up her seat, quietly insisting that she be respected, set all kinds of things in motion," she said.

"You know who else is my shero?" she asked?

"Your what?!" I proclaimed.

"My shero. The same thing as a hero but with a she in the front."

I nodded. My sisters had used the same word.

"Mary McLeod Bethune," she continued. "You know that woman was born into a slave family, walked four miles to school when she was a girl, created a school in Florida for African-American girls all by herself, campaigned for black women to vote when black men couldn't even vote and stood up to the Ku Klux Klan to boot! A lot of people don't know this but it was Franklin Roosevelt's mother, Sara Roosevelt, who invited her to some big political society lunch. She was the only black woman there in a roomful of white women but Mrs. Roosevelt gave her the place of honor at the table and introduced her to the president's wife Eleanor. Hmmm, and that was the beginning. Mary McLeod Bethune and Eleanor Roosevelt began to stir the pot. I've always wanted to be like her.

"She said a lot of meaningful things but I think one of my favorite quotes of hers was, *There is a place in God's sun for the youth 'farthest down' who has the vision, the determination, and the courage to reach it.*

She paused for a moment thinking about Mary Bethune's accomplishments and then she looked over at me, "You know she was a teacher, don't you?" and gave me that Mona Lisa smile.

Mary McLeod Bethune 1955
www.quotealbum.com

Frederick D. Jones • Sue Bowron

Historic White Hall, Bethune-Cookman University, Daytona Beach, Florida - The Florida College Guide

12 – Teaching

The centerpiece on the kitchen table had a glittery number 40 peeking out of the top. I couldn't grasp what significance the number 40 had to do with Mr. and Mrs. Thomas. The challenge blew through my brain, "Not his birthday. Not her birthday. Not Stephanie's birthday. Not their anniversary. Yes? No, their anniversary was number 45. Number of . . . "I gave up. I couldn't make an association with the number 40 surrounded by flowers. I stared at it like knowing that one fact would open the secrets of the universe. The number 40 in a floral display. 40. I didn't hear her when she came into the room and when she touched my sleeve, I nearly jumped out of my skin.

"What is it?" she asked. I tried to recover, embarrassed that I was so engrossed in the flowers that I had lost myself.

"It's nothing," I said trying to sound normal. "Pretty flowers."

"Aren't they?" she said. "They were the centerpieces at a 40th reunion banquet for Franklin Parish High School and I was their guest speaker last night." I rolled my eyes around. Of course, why couldn't I have thought of that? 'What other goofy thing are you going to fixate on?' I asked myself. It had been a long week and I was kind of punchy. I was looking for a place to live in Shreveport and had been driving back and forth from Baton Rouge to Shreveport to Winnsboro and last weekend I had driven up to Atlanta for two days to attend a conference. I need to sit down, I thought, so I did.

"You want something to drink?" she asked, a little concerned. I nodded and she went to the refrigerator for ice. "I've been trying to use that Facebook," she said, "Somebody said they liked me. I guess I like them, too, but I don't know what button to push to tell them." The ice clinked in the glass and she poured some iced tea out of a white plastic pitcher. "Are you all right?" she asked.

"Yes, I'm fine. Things have been on the fast track lately and I think I'm hitting a wall. I need to take a break. I'll be all right after a good night's sleep."

"Good, that's good," she murmured as she sat the glass down on the kitchen table along with a plate of Oreos. My diet had been overcome by more urgent issues lately and I welcomed the cookies along with a big gulp of sweet tea.

"Did you ever feel like giving up teaching?" I looked up at her. Her eyes narrowed and she looked at me with increasing uneasiness.

"No, I felt like whacking a few kids, though," she admitted. I laughed at the thought of little Mrs. Thomas trying to slap the tar out of some six-foot basketball player.

"Some of those kids never did get it. My greatest frustration was when I would try to explain something to somebody in simple language and they would look at you and say, 'What in the hell are you talking about?'"

I burst out laughing and felt the muscles in my body relax. I slumped back in my chair, glad to be in her kitchen listening to her stories.

"You know most people are trying to talk while you're talking and they don't get what you're saying. Some of those kids never learned how to listen. They don't even know why they're in school. If a student came into school to hide or sleep or be sick, you know what? You're in the wrong place, darling! This is a classroom and when you come in here, your brain and your mind have to belong to me. You have to listen to me. Otherwise, it isn't going to work.

"They came in with all kinds of excuses. Excuse me? Well, you know what that means. It means you have an F. You don't have your homework. You have nothing to turn in. What am I going to grade you on? Now, you think about that. What's more important to you? The job you have now or the one that you're trying to prepare for?" She was getting wound up. You really didn't want to be on her bad side.

"I would put my finger right in their face and tell them that you're the one putting the value on your education. I'm not. So you decide. I need to do my job.

"My frustration towards the end of my career was that kids are just no longer interested in school. I can't say they were unruly because they would listen to what I said, but they were not responding. They have to listen and be productive in class. They have to learn something. I didn't want them to drop out of school or just leave my class."

I took another cookie and listened closely. I hadn't heard her speak of the disappointing side of her work before.

"You know, when I first came to Franklin Parish in 1963 right after I graduated from college, I had been offered a job at a special school for children who worked the shrimping season with their parents. They would need to be off from school for weeks at a time and their school year wasn't matched with the normal calendar from September to May. Well, it turned out that these children were neither black, nor white; they were called mulatto. Today they're called bi-racial. There were eighteen of them and I could see it wasn't the kind of teaching opportunity I was hoping for. I didn't want to go back on my word because these children needed a teacher and I didn't know what to do.

Teaching in the 1960s

"Well, I got a call from Horace G. White who was principal of Franklin Parish Training School and he offered me a job as a biology teacher. When he saw how little I was, he asked me how I was going to teach all those big boys in my class. I told him that I was going to teach them and he said, 'You can't do nothing with them big boys.' And I said, 'You just watch me.'

"The first day of class, Mr. White was watching me. He didn't think I would be able to handle it. I walked into the classroom and those boys were just looking at me and I said, 'I dare you to say something.' After that, they were all just as sweet as they could be." I could see her staring down those big boys. She had done it to me.

"Of course, I learned how to teach from my own teachers. Mrs. Basby was my home economics teacher and she was the most influential person in my life. She was a real sweet person, and she had such a nice voice. She was always dressed to the nines. She would say, 'Mabel, come here and help me with this.' I didn't want to learn cooking because I'd rather be reading a book but when she got finished telling us about the importance of being a good homemaker, it was quite impressive. Anyway, I already knew how to cook because my mother taught each one of us.

"Mrs. Basby used to say, 'If you stay as sweet and pretty as you are, you probably won't even have to worry about cooking.'

"I was a little sassy and I said, 'Meaning somebody is going to get me a maid or something?'

"'No indeed, honey,' she replied. ' Your husband will cook for you every day.'

"'So it depends on what man I marry?' I asked her.

"'Yes,' she said. 'And I don't have any doubt that you're going to pick a good husband.'

"Well, as it turns out, the husband I've got sure doesn't cook."

We shared a knowing look and I asked her, "Did you model your teaching style after her?"

"In part, yes, and a few others. My music teacher was quite a woman. She knew her music. I didn't mind learning scales and music history, but I didn't want to be part of the choir. I didn't want to sing anything. She went to my parents and talked my daddy into paying for piano lessons but I didn't take them.

"'Girl,' she'd say, 'with all your smarts and your looks, you can have anything you want if you just go after it.'

"'Well,' I said, 'I don't want to sing.'

"And she told me, 'But you're going to sing in this choir.'
"So I said, 'Okay . . . if you say so, Mrs. Washington.' And I sang in the choir.

"She expected the best from me in class even if I didn't want to do it. And that's what I expected from the students I taught. I knew they weren't all going to be biology majors but I expected that they would come to class with respect for learning. I didn't want to be just a teacher. I wanted to be a special teacher because I always felt that a teacher should guide and lead people in a way that would make them able to help themselves and others. That you would teach them things that they didn't know and make them aware of things. That's what I always wanted to do and you know, Fred, I feel as though I accomplished that."

I stared down at the floor and told her what was on my heart, "I remember who the teacher was who impacted my life the most and it's the one I'm talking to now." She smiled broadly and I could see that she was accepting it for the gift I meant it to be.

To break the tension I kidded her, "You know, you weren't all that easy on me."

"No," she grinned, "I don't expect that I was. You know if I see something wrong being done, I'm going to say something. I try to explain things to people so they don't make the same mistake again."

"Yes," I replied, "I know. I remember one day I was doing something, I can't even remember what right now, but you came up to me and said, 'Frederick, if you play with a puppy, he'll lick your face.' I didn't know what it meant at the time but all I did know was that I had messed up."

"I don't know why when I have to reprimand people, they have to remember it so well," she laughed. "Now, of course, you can tell when I know and mean what I say. I don't know if it's my voice or the look that I give, but they knew."

"I think it's the look," I said, shaking my head. "It's the eyes. And your tone . . . you don't raise your voice. It's the look. You look a certain way and you say it with a level tone and it's like OH MY GOD." We both collapsed in laughter.

"You know," she said between giggles, "One time, after integration, I had this white boy in my class and he puffed up and said, 'My daddy's an attorney.' I gave him a look and he sat down and never said another word in my class. Lord, I must have been a terror because even the white kids knew what to do or say.

"I really enjoyed teaching. When it was time for me to leave, I just prayed on it and left. I knew that I would have problems with the next generation of children. I don't think I could have stayed in the classroom with the children that we are faced with today. I always respected my students and I expected the same thing from them.

"I've taught a lot of outstanding students. Some are now outstanding lawyers like you, doctors, nurses, preachers. I see a lot of my students even now and they say, 'Thank you, Mrs. Thomas, for being my teacher.' This is always rewarding for me because I feel in some small way, I contributed to their success."

Mabel Lawrence Thomas in Biology Class

She looked over at the 40th reunion flowers and they spoke to me of noisy hallways, quiet intense exam rooms, smelly lab experiments, homecoming queens, and beaming graduates. I saw myself in a chrysanthemum.

13 – Celebration

I arrived early at the Waterfront Grill to check on the final banquet arrangements. This event had been in the planning stages even before my departure from Atlanta and I was excited that the day had arrived. I had been in contact with a former classmate, Janice Powell who now lived in Tacoma, Washington, and she was helping financially. I went out front just as the limo was pulling up. Lorenzo Richardson, another classmate, was contributing his limousine services. He stepped out of the limo and opened the door with a flourish and took the hand of each woman who stepped out: Gracie Bolden, Dorothy Brown, Ida Hoard, and Dorothy Parker Swayzer. He was comical in his exaggerated chivalry and the women loved it. I led the ladies and their husbands into the private room and Lorenzo jumped into his limo to fetch more guests.

As people arrived, I did a mental check to make sure everyone was there. Social gatherings always have their natural patterns. In one corner were the men: Otis Thomas, Eli Brown, Leroy Scott, and Deacue Fields in earnest conversation. Politics, probably, I thought. Mordessa Corbin was seated at the table and talking with Mrs. Thomas, Helen Crawford, and Marria Fields. Near the door were my own beautiful sisters, teachers all: Emma Blackshire, Georgia Jones, and Louise Johnson. There were speeches, toasts, and laughs and quicker than I could imagine, the evening was over.

Left to Right - Georgia Jones, Louise Jones Johnson, Gracie Tolliver Bolden, Marria Fields, Dorothy Jane Parker Swayzer, Otis Thomas, Deacue Fields, Jr., Leroy Scott (tall man in the back), Mabel Lawrence Thomas, Eli Brown, Jr. Mordessa Richardson Corbin, Dorothy Wright Brown, Ida Hoard at the Celebrate Teaching banquet.

A few weeks later I moved into my new office in the old Waggonner Building in Shreveport to prepare for the launch of the Judge Paul Pressler School of Law and I found myself surrounded with the same boxes I had packed in Kennesaw. Just as I had predicted months ago, the unpacking would be as frustrating as the packing because of my disorganized haste. However, I took my time and lined up books on the shelves and organized my files. I had brought my hammer and picture hangers with me and I hung my degrees on the wall. I carefully unwrapped framed photographs of my sons and my parents and placed them on my desk. Then I reached into my briefcase for a recent photograph of me and Mrs. Thomas taken in her backyard. I placed it with the other photographs and looked around at my degrees, my law books, and my office. I was doing more than I actually dreamed was possible because of God's rich gifts in my parents and in the teacher who persistently challenged me to do my very best. Her words were still fresh in my mind, "Fred Jones, if you play with a puppy, it will lick your face." I looked down at my hands and then at the ceiling and smiled thinking, "God, I wish I knew what she meant by that."

I took a moment and bowed my head in prayer, "Gracious Father, thank you for where I am right at this moment. Thank you for this opportunity. And Father, I thank you most of all for the people who helped me get here – for my parents, my teachers, and for Mrs. Thomas. Lord, for all the puppies that have licked my face, I thank you for the ones named Love, Faith, Commitment, Education, and Friendship. Let them crawl up in my lap and may I embrace them all the days of my life."

Mabel Lawrence Thomas and Frederick Jones

Appendix

Mabel Lawrence Thomas was elected Teacher of the Year of Winnsboro High School 1989-1990 and Teacher of the Year for Franklin Parish for the school year of 1989-1990. She was also awarded the Congressman Jerry Huckaby Pursuit of Excellence Teacher of the Year certificate.

Mabel Lawrence Thomas, Louisiana Congressman Jerry Huckaby, and Mary Ann Beasley at the Pursuit of Excellence Teacher of the Year Awards

After winning these local and regional awards, she submitted her application for the 1990 National Teacher of the Year award. Below are excerpts from her application packet, which gives insight into her professional career.

Professional Biography

I was born in New Orleans, Louisiana to the late Noles and Lillie Lawrence, the fourth of eight children. Because of their limited education (eighth grade), my parents were motivated to elevate the educational level of their children. At the age of three, my mother taught me to read and write. I started a school of my own with my family and in the evenings, everyone had to read and write as I instructed them to do.

At the age of five, I taught my fifty-one year old grandmother to read and write. Her inability to read and write was kept hidden from her grandchildren until she became a student of my school. I discovered this when she could not perform her assignments, so I set out to teach her to read. I made alphabet cards to help her recognize and write the alphabet. Then we proceeded to write words. She was very excited and proud when she was able to write her name. This was such an accomplishment that she was ready and willing to learn how to read and would read every evening until she was able to read.

My greatest joy and feeling of accomplishment was seeing my grandmother sign her name instead of using the letter X to denote her signature. I knew that I had caused a learning process.

My formal teaching experience began in September 1963. I was hired by the Franklin Parish School Board as a biology teacher at the former Franklin Parish Training School. I was later transferred to Winnsboro High School during the unification process of Franklin Parish Schools and am presently a biology and general science teacher.

My greatest accomplishment in education is contributing to the education of outstanding and productive students that are involved in the area of science. Some of these students are Dr. Dewitt Patterson, who is practicing medicine; Vanessa Brass Brown, who is supervisor of nurses at St. Francis Medical Center; Diane Leonard, who is supervisor of nurses in the Intensive Care Unit at St. Francis Medical Center; and Renita Singleton Benjamin, who is a medical technician at North Monroe Community Hospital.

I am presently working with five of my former students: Velma Neal Brown, who is teaching aerospace science and general science and who also serves as assistant principal of Winnsboro High School; Theresa Heath, who is teaching biology and chemistry; Mike Clay, who is teaching mathematics; and Dorothy Swayzer and Kenneth Blackson, who have taught science but are presently teaching English and business, respectively. I am very proud of these young educators.

Professional Development Activities

I received my early childhood education in the Plaquemine Parish School System. I graduated as Valedictorian of my elementary and high school graduating classes. I attended school for twelve years with perfect attendance.

I earned a Bachelor of Science Degree in Biology and General Science and a Master's Degree in Biology Education from Southern University, Baton Rouge, Louisiana. I have done further studies at Northeast Louisiana University Monroe and at Louisiana State University Eunice.

I completed all requirements for the Professional Improvement Program (PIP). These courses included:
- Effective Teaching
- Fire Safety
- Multicultural Education
- Aviation
- Workshops:
- Energy Education
- Plant Identification
- Critical Elements of Teaching
- Modifying Instructions to Improve Thinking

I am a member of the National Education Association, Louisiana Association of Educators, Franklin Parish

Education Association, and a former member of the National Biology Teachers Association.

I have served as a member of the state evaluation committee for the evaluation of Downsville High School. I have served as facilitator of the Franklin Parish Workshop for Science Teachers and have served as chairman of the Science Department of Winnsboro High School. Furthermore, I have served as sponsor of the Science Club. The Science Club has been actively engaged in many activities which climax each year with an educational tour to such places as Atlanta, Georgia; Washington, D.C.; Orlando, Florida; Hot Springs, Arkansas; and Huntsville, Alabama. In conclusion, I served as a senior sponsor in addition to being a sponsor for the Pep Squad and Cheerleaders.

Community Involvement

I am a member of St. Mary's Catholic Church and have served as a catechism teacher. I am presently serving as a lector during Sunday masses. I have served on the finance committee for the church. I have also participated in fund raising activities such as selling tickets for raffles and barbecue suppers and holding rummage sales. I am presently being evaluated to become a member of the Catholic Daughters of the Americas, an organization whose goal is to raise awareness and a consciousness about various issues, especially the needy.

I am a member of the Modern Matrons, a civic and social organization which has sponsored many civic and social activities that add culture to the community. In the interest of education, the Matrons have participated in many school related activities and issued several scholarships to deserving high school graduates. The Matrons most recently sponsored Project Excellence, a tutorial program that is held after school in local churches to assist students who are weak in certain subject areas. I served as a coordinator in planning the program and also assisted in tutoring in the science classes.

I do volunteer work by assisting the elderly in my community by taking them to visit their doctor and to shop. There are also times that I shop for them.

I also serve as wedding consultant and coordinator for many young ladies in my community. I have sponsored many wedding showers and debutante teas honoring many outstanding young ladies.

I have also served as a fund raiser for the Wheels for Life – St. Jude's Children's Hospital, by holding a Fun Day at the community park. The activities included selling from concession stands, a softball tournament, and collecting donations. I have served as a door to door solicitor for the March of Dimes and Easter Seals Associations.

Frederick D. Jones • Sue Bowron

Philosophy of Teaching

As a teacher, I am committed to the education of children. I, in every way, try to serve as a role model and to exemplify the professionalism of teaching.

I feel that a good teacher is one that exhibits the following characteristics:

A teacher should have a sincere desire to help develop the minds of children. A good teacher is one who recognizes the needs of a child and does everything in his power to fulfill that need through special assistance, homework assignments, and nurturing when the need arises.

A teacher should be well qualified and knowledgeable in his chosen area of study. A good teacher should be open-minded and always have a quest for knowledge not only in his chosen area but in related areas as well.

A teacher should be patient, fair, honest, and understanding. A good teacher should allow students to absorb, realize, and apply the knowledge that is presented to him. Each student should be expected to perform to his potential and be evaluated accordingly.

A teacher should be willing to put forth that extra effort to go beyond the call of duty. There should be conferences with students before or after class to motivate and assist them with problems that may be affecting their performances in class. If this does not help, a parent-teacher conference should be arranged.

A teacher should have a continuing desire to learn. A good teacher should keep abreast of the latest trends in his chosen area by reading current materials from professional magazines, newspapers, and pamphlets.

My philosophy of teaching is and always will be that teaching causes one to learn. If the atmosphere is conducive to learning and materials are presented in a perceivable manner, reinforced, and evaluated, there is no doubt that some learning will take place. All students who are educable will learn something from a good teacher. I feel that the bridge between intelligence and ignorance is the teacher. A good teacher is one that teaches the whole child by, in addition to presenting subject matter, presenting skills practical to everyday living. If the bridge between ignorance and intelligence is structured well, one can successfully pass inability to ability.

My greatest reward is knowing that I have, in some small way, helped to shape the minds of many young, productive people.

Frederick D. Jones • Sue Bowron

Education Issues and Trends

I think that the major issues of public education today are: 1) a lack of parents' participation in their children's education; 2) drugs and alcohol abuse, and 3) dropouts.

I feel that the reasons for a lack of parental participation in structuring their children's education are 1) parents are not educated; 2) parents are not truly concerned with the education of their children, and 3) parents have no control over their children.

As a result, most children do not get the best education available to them. They realize too late in life the true value of a good education and blame everyone but themselves. This attitude is nourished throughout life and affects everyone.

To improve the concern and participation of parents in the educational system, I feel that a well-organized active parent organization should be formed to assist school administrators and teachers in promoting the philosophy and goals of the school. There should also be a means for parents and teachers to communicate either through a parent-teacher organization or an open conference session.

Parents should mandate that a particular time be designated as study time, for each child without any distractions (such as telephone, TV, etc.). A check should be made to see if homework is done and that it is according to guidelines.

Parents should be included in every phase of the education of their children. Encouragement and motivation should occur throughout a child's life. If parents would encourage their children to do better, the children will realize that education is a very important part of their lives.

Personal Teaching Style

The innovative instructional methods that I have successfully used with my students are:

Challenging students to use their abilities to make a mental picture of what they hear and read for easy recall.

- Using instructional games or puzzles that are related to the unit of study.
- Using transparencies with interesting pictures or characters to illustrate an important concept.
- Using problems or situations that require critical thinking to encourage students to use a scientific approach.
-

I have often shared these ideas and others with many of my coworkers and fellow teachers. During our departmental meetings, we usually share new ideas and techniques.

Frederick D. Jones • Sue Bowron

The Teaching Profession

Would you recommend that your most capable students enter the teaching profession?

Yes, I would recommend that my most capable students enter the teaching profession. Today, there is a dire need for teachers and I often remind my students of this dilemma and encourage them to consider this most important field of endeavor.

To me, teaching is most rewarding in that you feel such joy and gratification in knowing that you have helped someone who thought that it could not be done. It is such a thrill to see the look of accomplishment and the sparkle in a student's eyes when he has accomplished a task.

Teaching will always be an active profession, in spite of the new techniques, such as computerized teaching and satellite teaching. Nothing can take the place of a classroom teacher, for a classroom teacher provides the direct contact that is necessary for immediate growth, the caring and concern that a machine cannot provide.

Teachers prepare the world. They motivate, cultivate, and educate those persons who may become or are our presidents, prime ministers, politicians, doctors, lawyers, religious leaders, laborers, and yes, the teacher also.

Yes, I do recommend that my capable students enter the teaching profession.

What would you do to assist teachers in becoming exemplary?

To assist teachers in becoming a good role model, I would encourage them to be respectful to their students. In order to be respected, one must first show respect for himself. This is an abstract quality, which comes from within and is reflected in one's appearance and actions at school, at home, and in the community.

A teacher should take pride in whatever he attempts to do. If he approaches his work with pride and enthusiasm, this will take shape in motivating his students.

In our society, children are "crying out" for role models. Because the teacher spends quite a bit of the day with the student, he can be, and should be, a role model.

If a child feels that he is "cared for" or "is somebody," it makes the job of teaching easier. The good teacher must have a love for children, be patient, and be a dedicated worker and role model.

To what extent do you think teachers should be accountable for the outcomes of their students?

As a teacher, one should be accountable for the outcome of his students in the following ways:

Teaching basic skills as mandates so that students may be able to perform these skills when called upon to do so and be able to apply these skills where applicable. When the mandated basic skills are taught and students are motivated to do their best; it is his responsibility to perform satisfactorily. However, if a certain percentage of the students in a class fail to perform satisfactorily, it is the teacher's responsibility to re-teach and re-evaluate.

It is the teacher's responsibility to prepare students to be independent thinkers and doers. A good teacher presents thought-provoking ideas through given situations and by means of visual aids.

Teachers should prepare students to be responsible and productive individuals in society. This should encourage students to know themselves, be proud of themselves, and be the very best that they can be.

National Teacher of the Year

As National Teacher of the Year, I would exhibit the professionalism of being a teacher in every situation that I may encounter by thinking scientifically and sound and in every way try to express ideas that would represent all teachers.

My message to America would certainly include the cry, "Children First!" I would appeal to administrators, teachers, and parents to let their first concern be the education of the children that everyone involved — administrators, teachers, and parents — be organized into a strong body to promote education on all levels. We need to support taxes that would provide more and necessary materials for class instructions. We must promote efficiency in the classroom, increase salaries for teachers, and dedicate the responsibilities of basic home training to parents.

I would encourage parents to be more concerned with their children's education and to take an active, sincere part in structuring their education for the future.

A second way to provide the best opportunity for all children to get a good education is to offer two curriculums in every high school — an academic and a vocational curriculum. I feel that this would give every student an opportunity to better prepare for his chosen vocation.

Letters of Recommendation

September 8, 1989

To Whom It May Concern:

I have served on the Winnsboro High School faculty with Mrs. Mabel Thomas for over ten years and as her principal since the fall of 1988. I have always found Mrs. Thomas to be a teacher who was ready to assist with extracurricular activities and other duties as necessary.

Mrs. Thomas has served our school well as the Winnsboro High School Science Club Sponsor, the chairman of the Winnsboro High School Science Department, and as a senior class sponsor. The WHS Science Club has been an actively engaged club with numerous activities which climax each year with a science-related tour. The club has eagerly looked forward to the spring trip each year. Mrs. Thomas has taken the club to Hot Springs, Arkansas; Washington, D.C.; Orlando, Florida; and Huntsville, Alabama.

Mrs. Thomas is a caring, dedicated teacher who is appreciated and respected by students, parents, and teachers. She has the outstanding ability of communicating her concern for students to them as well as to others.

Through a Teacher's Eyes

It is with pride that the faculty of Winnsboro High School elected Mrs. Mabel Thomas, 1989-90 Winnsboro High School Teacher of the Year. We are confident that after you review her portfolio, you will agree that she is an outstanding teacher.

Sincerely,
John R. Sartin
Principal

September 8, 1989

To Whom It May Concern:

I have known Mrs. Mabel Thomas for several years and have always found her to be an outstanding individual. We met in a teacher/student relationship, when I was a student at Winnsboro High School. I found her to be one of the most qualified teachers I had ever known. She so inspired me as a student, I wanted to become a teacher. Today I am teaching the same subject in which she sparked my interest several years ago.

To me an excellent teacher is one who can bring a subject matter to life and challenge students to do their best. Mrs. Thomas has that ability.

I now have the privilege of teaching with Mrs. Thomas. She has many great qualities that attributed to her being elected Winnsboro High School's Teacher of the Year.

Respectfully,
Theresa Heath

The Family Tree of Mabel Lawrence Thomas

True to her word, Mrs. Thomas keeps a detailed list of family birthdays and anniversaries. Here, she pays tribute to those she holds most dear.

My Grandparents

My paternal grandparents were:

Issac Lawrence born March 27, 1841 and died on June 12, 1917.

Amelia Johnson Lawrence was born on December 5, 1843 and died on October 25, 1928. They were married on November 12, 1859 in Plaquemines Parish, Sarah, Louisiana.

My maternal grandparents were:

Leonard James was born on December 13, 1882 and died on February 14, 1942.

Louvenia Simmons James was born on May 16, 1870 and died on May 19, 1975. They were married on December 12, 1920 in Plaquemines Parish, Oakville, Louisiana.

Frederick D. Jones • Sue Bowron

My Parents

Noles Lawrence was born on December 25, 1913 to Issac Lawrence and Amelia Johnson Lawrence. He died on May 7, 1983.

Lillie James Lawrence was born on December 5, 1916 to Leonard James and Louvenia Simmons James. She died on October 27, 1984. They were married on November 12, 1932.

My Siblings
(Listed in order of birth)

Brother – Noles Lawrence, Jr. He married Emma at an early age and they had three children: Noles, III; Adrell; and Leonard. After Emma's death, he married Gwendolyn who had two sons from a previous marriage, Chevalier and Chenault, increasing his family to five children. He died June 14, 2010.

Sister – Julia Lawrence Homer. She and her husband Ernest had eight children: Ernest, Jr. (deceased); Vernon and Verna (twins); Anthony, Wendell, Colleen and Collette (twins); and Bernadine. Ernest died in 1990 and Julia died in January 2008.

Sister – Lillie Rose Lawrence Hill. She and her husband Felton (deceased) had seven children: Felton, Jr. (deceased); Lavene; Byron; David and Dauetta (twins);

Sonya LaNeka (deceased); and Sherman Issac. Lillie Rose now lives in Texas and is raising her granddaughter, Morgan.

Me – Mabel Lawrence Thomas was born on March 29, 1940 and married Otis Thomas on June 12, 1965.

Brother – James Lawrence, Sr. married Velma at an early age and they have one son, James, Jr. He later married Bartainer. He now lives in Lafayette near his son.

Brother – Freddy Lawrence, Sr., the "intellect of the family," has two post graduate degrees from Purdue University. He is married to Margaret and they have a son, Freddy, Jr., and a daughter, Francine. They live in Baton Rouge, Louisiana.

Brother – Sherman Lawrence, Sr. is married to Ina and they have four children: Sharon; Sherman, Jr.; Christine; and Gennie. They are living in New Orleans, Louisiana.

Sister – Leah Lawrence Watson. She and her ex-husband Larry have one son, Larry, Jr. Leah now lives in Texas near her son and his family.

Made in the USA
Lexington, KY
15 April 2012